BARBARA PYM

Barbara with Philip Larkin.
'He's shy but very responsive and jokey. Hilary took our photo together.' 1977

BARBARA PYM

A Passionate Force

Ann Allestree

Book Guild Publishing

Sussex, England

First published in Great Britain in 2015 by
The Book Guild Ltd
The Werks
45 Church Road
Hove, BN3 2BE

Typesetting in Garamond by
YHT Ltd, London

Printed and bound in Great Britain by
CPI Group (UK) Ltd, Croydon, CR0 4YY

A catalogue record for this book is available from
The British Library.

ISBN 978 1 910298 51 0

Contents

Foreword

You may have walked behind her in the streets of Pimlico, or Kilburn or High Holborn; the old haunts where she lived and worked. A tall woman in sensible shoes and a belted white mackintosh. Her thick brown hair is cut short. A pixie hood would not be out of place in drizzle. She holds her head high as though such detachment must give space for thought and observation.

Her face lights up. An acquaintance? She approaches the deep wide display window of a well-loved bookshop. She comes closer and we see her reflection on the glass; a blurred half smile steals over the refined face. She turns and settles herself on the seat beside a bus stop, her string bag on her lap with a library book and a supper for one. From her handbag she retrieves a spiral notebook. She looks up sharply, with piercing grey eyes intent on the passing crowd; the huddled bent figure, the young couple, the old nun – and "the things people say:

I never read novels
I never eat jam
I'm not a great lover of music
No, it just passes the time"

She makes her idiosyncratic notes in a neat hand.
She is our heroine. She is Barbara Pym; 1913–1980

1

The Sister's Story

A few miles to the north west of Oxford lies Finstock, a Cotswold village with medieval foundations. The slate-roofed stone cottages and barns, skirted with drystone walls, straggle down to a wooded valley. The ancient pubs and manor houses, with scattered traces of a Roman villa beyond, remain vestiges of the ancient woollen industry. The sloping fields are thick with sheep; badger, deer and fox roam at will, with some left pitiable and dead by roadsides. Villagers stride out with dogs; others are lured to The Plough Inn for steak and kidney pudding beside a cavernous log fire.

Barn Cottage, the home shared by Barbara Pym and her sister Hilary from 1972, had originally been converted from a 17th Century wheelwright's workshop. Small and snug with a large open fire, it had a beam in every room. There was the additional bonus of a double garage. This invaluable space was storage for furniture accrued from the sisters' larger London homes. The steep terraced garden is a profusion of flowering shrubs and berries, approached up through little stone steps and grass footways. On a winter's day, twenty-two years after Pym's death in 1980, the beds are still pulsing with young shoots and buds. Clematis coils round the front door and a chunky fig hugs the wall.

Hilary lets me in with a cheerful smile. She has arthritis and walks with a stick. She settles down and talks to me about her elder sister Barbara Pym.

"I was never conscious of her writing and she always carried these spiral pocket notebooks and would jot down random ideas and observations as they came to her. My favourite book? It must be *Less than Angels* with its slant on the anthropologists. You know people are obsessed with the idea that Barbara wrote only about clergymen. As children, in Oswestry, we were involved with church activities." Their mother, Irena (neé Spenser Thomas) was born in Oswestry and became assistant organist at the parish church of St Oswald. Their father, Frederic, sang bass in the choir.

"Young curates often came to supper," Hilary continued. "I remember being smitten by a handsome new curate. I was fourteen. He was talking with my mother and his legs were crossed. I could see the white combinations showing under his cassock." Hilary's strange, emotive moment was immortalised in the opening lines of Barbara's first novel, *Some Tame Gazelle*.

The new curate seemed quite a nice young man, but what a pity it was that his combinations showed, tucked carelessly into his socks, when he sat down. Belinda had noticed it when they had met him for the first time at the vicarage last week and had felt quite embarrassed.

"Our mother was active in the parish and a member of the WI. She even bought a motorbike in the war to get around. She was not a boyish person – just practical. We had ponies too and chickens."

Did their mother feed the chickens in an old tweed coat? Like Barbara's heroine, Jane Cleveland, in her novel *Jane and Prudence*?

Jane put on an old tweed coat which hung in the hall – the kind of coat one might have used for feeding the chickens in . . .

"Yes, the analogy was apt" murmured Hilary.

Their father, Frederic Crampton Pym, was illegitimate. His mother, Phoebe Pym, had worked as a maid at Poundisford Park, Pitminster, Somerset, the family home of Edmund Bourdillon. The Cramptons from Ireland were close friends and would often stay. It was supposed that Phoebe had a liaison with a member of this family. A supposition further borne out by Frederic Crampton Pym himself in giving the name to his two daughters. Barbara never knew of these revelations. It was only after her death in 1980, that Hilary had undertook the research. It had always been assumed that the family was descended from the early seventeenth puritan parliamentarian, John Pym. Their mother's family had a steady provenance of border-land farmers, whose ancestry harked back to the early Welsh kings.

"Father was good-hearted and appreciative, never demanding and always pleased to see us at his office in Oswestry. He was well set up with his own solicitor's practice. Both our parents were athletic. My mother had been a keen hockey player and father used to run. They became good golfers. And in my teens I played golf well." Was Barbara athletic? Hilary chuckled. "Not a bit. I came across an old school magazine from our Liverpool College. In a reminiscence of old girls, Barbara was even dismissed as 'clumsy'."

The sisters had a happy, uncomplicated childhood. Their home, Morda Lodge, was a solid redbrick Edwardian manse and had a large garden. Over the wall, at 'Scotswood' lived their maternal grandmother and Aunts May and Janie. Their mother also had another sister, Nellie, married with four children, who lived in Middlesex. They would all come and stay at Christmas and Easter. "With our parents members of the Oswestry Operatic Society we children were encouraged to act and sing; Gilbert and Sullivan mostly." Aged nine years Barbara wrote an operetta – 'The Magic Diamond' – complete with a wizard, a king and a queen and a princess with two princes and a flower girl called Violet. Aunt Nellie Selway and the lively Selway cousins helped stage the production.

'The profits (if any) will be given to the waifs and strays' – added a beneficent touch to the programme. And so it was that on an evening in April 1922 the scene was set for Act One in the 'King's Garden'.

"My mother also induced in us a love of reading. She herself especially liked novels. But I remember her reading mostly Saki's short stories to us."

Barbara was 12 years when she was sent off to board at Liverpool College, Huyton. Hilary was shocked by this sudden deprivation of her sister's company. She had waited by the front gate the whole day, anguishing for her return. She and her mother would take the train from Oswestry to see Barbara. Visiting was rationed to once a month. Hilary was soon to follow and laments that they were 'incarcerated'. Their clever and culture conscious mother, with her zeal for hockey, had felt the day school at Oswestry an inadequate challenge for her daughters. Their subsequent achievements in the disciplined confines at Huyton were average, although Barbara did become Chairman of the Literary Society. She was reading avidly; the detective stories of Edgar Wallace were notable favourites, Kipling, poetry and at sixteen years, she fell on the author who first inspired her to write herself. She discovered Aldous Huxley.

From childhood Barbara and Hilary had a deeply intuitive rapport, devoid of sibling envy. After the war, with their mother dead and their father re-married, they shared homes for the rest of their lives. Hilary had started secretarial work with the BBC which evolved into her permanent career of thirty-two years. In 1946 Barbara had been offered work at the International African Institute in Fetter Lane, under the aegis of the anthropologist, Professor Daryll Forde. And they shared the cats and the cooking and the kitchen sink. Tatiana, a ravishing tortoiseshell, petted and capricious, had been immortalised as 'Faustina' in *An Unsuitable Attachment*. Tom Boilkin, her companion, was handsome, black and white and would lop through the front window dangling a mouse. Minerva, a more placid tortoiseshell, sus-tained a good life of eighteen years. Called 'Nana' by the sisters she too had her capers. She mesmerised television viewers of 'Tea with Miss Pym' by landing on the tea tray, her paw perilously posed above the milk jug. This select party took place in the garden of Barn Cottage, when Lord David Cecil conducted an arch and amusing interview of Barbara. After Minerva's death, a stray tabby slipped into her place. 'Mother' soon redeemed the feral status quo with four tom kittens. The sisters kept Justin and gave away his three siblings – 'But mother went missing and Justin was run over . . .' Hilary became distressed at the memory of it all.

Did Hilary remember the times that Philip Larkin came to tea? In July 1976 he had taken a photograph of the sisters by the cottage door. And in April 1977 he had been asked to lunch; a meal proudly noted by Barbara in her diary:

23 April, Philip Larkin to lunch. We had sherry and then the wine (burgundy) Bob gave me for Christmas (was this rather insensitive to Bob?). We ate kipper pâté, then veal done with peppers and tomatoes, pommes Anna and celery and cheese (he didn't eat any Brie and we thought perhaps he only likes plain food). He's shy but very responsive and jokey. Hilary took our photo together and he left about 3.30, in his large Rover car (pale tobacco brown).

Hilary found him an extraordinary mixture. 'Playing all those women admirers along and carrying on that school-boyish smut with Kingsley

Amis.' Elizabeth Jane Howard recalled in later years that Larkin had 'the most beautiful smile and could be majestically courteous' (*Sunday Times News Review* 23 June 2002). There had been no romance between Larkin and Barbara, Hilary hastened to assure me. (Their prodigious letter-writing had extended nearly twenty years). Physically plain and extremely tall, Larkin had maintained close relationships with three women. They were a carefully sized-up coterie. His secretary, bright-eyed and bushy tailed, was 'the practical one', his librarian colleague was 'the romantic one'; fun and vivacious, she was party to a drink with Larkin and his fellow professors. But it was Monica Jones, 'the intellectual one', who surpassed them all and stood to inherit his modest house in Hull. ('I have bought an ugly little house, fearfully dear,' he had written to Barbara in 1974). Hilary remembered Monica Jones on her rare visits with Larkin to Barn Cottage. "She was dark and always wore dark glasses. One day she arrived in the village in a pink dress and a black hat. She looked bizarre." Perhaps it was that marked idiosyncrasy that had appealed to Larkin. He was a confirmed agnostic. It was the final supreme irony that his favourite muse, Monica Jones, should divide the bulk of her one million pound estate between St Paul's Cathedral, Durham Cathedral and Hexham Abbey. "Philip Larkin was a multi-faceted man," concluded Hilary. Others have described him as 'compartmentalised'.

When it came to sharing homes, the sisters were eminently compatible. Hilary conceded that Barbara was the better cook. Their first flat was in Pimlico, alongside St Gabriel's of Warwick Square. From 1949 they spent twelve years in spacious rooms on the first floor of a villa in Barnes. Their neighbour over the garden wall was the unctuous Mr Raymond of the Revue Bar. Hilary had an abiding memory of Paul Raymond. 'Looking out of the window I saw this tall, balding, academic-looking man carrying an ostrich feather boa around his garden.' In the Times Diary 19 August 1985, Hilary's story was published. She won a bottle of champagne for 'stories about the famous before they became well known.'

In 1961 the sisters moved to a Victorian house in Queen's Park, NW London. Here they had their own garden and kept three cats, much to the distaste of Barbara's young Bahamian admirer. His aversion was portrayed in *'The Sweet Dove Died'*, where he identified paw marks on the sink and cats' hair wafting through the air. The counterpart heroine was equally unnerved.

'The cats would be in and out of the room and Leonora would try to avoid getting one on her lap kneading at her skirt with its claws.' Leonora's hostess had been plucked so consistently that her clothes gave a bouclé effect. On Hilary's retirement in 1971 from the BBC, she bought Barn Cottage in Finstock. Barbara's own retirement from the International African Institute, incurred by the onset of her illness, came in 1974. Barn Cottage was to be their last home.

2

Intoxicating Oxford

Strictures of boarding school and a regulated teenage upbringing in the country were soon eclipsed by Barbara's arrival at Oxford. She went up to St Hilda's College in 1931 to read English literature. Aged eighteen years she was pitched into a new and heady world of academia – and men. A tall girl at 5′ 8″ and delicately built, Barbara cut an elegant figure and had beautiful hands; she was proud of her thick, brown wavy hair which despite the vicissitudes of her illness in old age always retained its colour. She had hazel-grey eyes and a broad smile, to reveal the strongest white teeth. The imperceptible protrusion of her left front tooth rather enhanced her appeal. Francis King, the novelist, once described her to me as 'healthy-looking'. As he had sat opposite her for the Booker Prize dinner at Claridge's, just two years before she died, the premise that Barbara Pym always retained her youthful good looks is borne out.

The agreeable preponderance of men over women undergraduates proved a kick-start to Barbara's self-identity. She became extrovert and feted; exuberant in debate and chased for her wit as much as her good looks and flawless complexion. She was a popular girl to reckon with. Her room on the top floor of St Hilda's overlooked the drive; a room with a view as to become a prerequisite in all her homes, as a source for novelistic material. She would talk long into the night with her fellow students, all equally intoxicated by their own verbosity. Smoking and drinking coffee and playing the gramophone, they held forth and raved rapturously. In *Oxford University Chest*, John Betjeman referred to tales of 'Cocoa Crushes' in women's colleges, but regretted that such wild allusions had never been substantiated. Barbara had decorated her room with inordinate attention to detail; having adopted 'Sandra' as a pseudonym, she embroidered it on her cushions and any favoured evening wear. To Barbara the name had the allure of East Europe aristocracy; it had a 'fast', romantic ring. A doll, 'wellerina' was another prop to adorn the scene. Barbara's succinct record in her diary – October 6, 1933 – is almost a pointer to descriptions as found in (Huxley's) *Crome Yellow*.

> I'm terribly enamoured of my new room, and have it most artistic and aesthetic. Chaste green for my bed – check cushions – beautiful pictures – books and bookends – bronze golden chrysanthemums on the table in the window alcove. I hear Magdalen and Merton clocks all the time.

Her first admirer was the dashing Adonis, Rupert Gleadow, a Wykhamist; brilliant and a perfect consort for those tentative first steps towards love and dalliance. His profile thrilled her; walking together, talking, punting and picnicking, she would steal a wily glance. With trepidation she invited him home in the summer vacation; Rupert's background was incomparably more sophisticated than her own. His conciliatory praise for Oswestry underlined his serious interest in her. Barbara was next introduced to his talkative mother over lunch at the Randolph. Perhaps symptomatic of his mother's approval, Rupert had attempted to seduce Barbara the following day – 'and he with all his charm, eloquence and masculine wiles, persuaded . . .' Here in her original diary pages have been remorselessly torn out. Barbara was adept at consigning any such diary entries of personal prime endeavour. She had never matched Rupert in his deeper feelings. She had felt more constrained to mother him; to put her arms around him when he shivered in the pouring Oxford rain. Intensely attracted to him, she kept in touch, eventually becoming friends with his wife, Helen. By April 1932, Barbara's diary had been full of Rupert Gleadow; he lavished every attention on her, to include a letter written in orange ink. On October 20th, five days after he had plied her with a 'colossal' tea in his rooms, with pleadings to let him make love to her, Barbara merely noted that they went to a film and "then went back to Rupert's digs before we had supper, and spent a generally happy and peaceful time, if I remember it rightly." A cooling period took over in the autumn, with such desultory entries as "I spent the afternoon with Rupert but can't remember what I did." On Sunday October 30th: "Sweet Rupert called for me …", and on Sunday November 6th: "I spent a few pleasant hours with Rupert in his digs. After tea 'till supper. Can't remember much else." By November, Barbara's work schedule appears to have superseded thoughts of Rupert. Monday November 7th: "Attended lectures and did a lot of work." Tuesday November 8th: "work".

Pym divided her studies at the Bodleian Library, between the dark rich interior of the 14th Century Duke Humfrey's reading room and the second floor upper reading room for English Literature; a lofty enfilade of rooms encompassing three sides of the Bodley quadrangle; brightly lit it is adorned with an early 17th Century frieze of 200 'Uomini famosi'. The austere high arched Gothic windows are studded with richly stained glass panels and look over an unparalleled view of Oxford's golden spires; a battery of pinnacles, battlemented parapets and balusters and distant towers are ranged around the adjacent bulk of the domed Radcliffe Camera. "Bod. in the afternoon, but I did no work. 'Lorenzo' was there." Her diary had become her confidant. "Love! Love! Love! Do the dons know how it affects our work – I wonder?" Pym was the first to recognise the tug between love and work. A weekly essay had to be produced to her tutor at St Hilda's; a disciplinary balance to the lectures and reading that she much preferred. She relished the idiosyncratic turn of events; her diary notes on September 26th, 1933: "What funny things one does – I finish an essay on 'The Puritanism of Spenser and Milton' and then dash off to the Regal with Dor to see *42nd Street* which was good – all legs and music." A disappointing lecture to Pym meant only one decent looking man present out of 30. But when her favourite tutor warned his audience that De Toqueville had not been able to write his book on The French Revolution, Pym had muttered 'Thank Heaven', for all to hear. The tutor had looked at her "with an expression of hurt and surprise on his dear face". Her cavalier dismissal of De Toqueville spelt failure in her 'Pass Moderations', the examination for first term undergraduates ("DeToqueville was my downfall.")

Pym's passion for research, for people and places, sprang from her Oxford education. Dipping into *Crockford's Clerical Directory*, Kelly's Street Directories, *Who's Who* and with time spent in libraries, she was motivated into her future writing. Oxford had a fundamental bearing on her books, reflected in her feelings and attitudes. Stored with her papers at the Bodleian is an evocative chronicle – 'her "work" – "NON FRUSTRA VIXI" (I have not lived in vain) – the motto of St Hilda's.

"A record of the adventures of the celebrated Barbara McPym during the year 1932/33 (written by herself)." It is an exuberant exposé of her Oxford life and loves. The former schoolgirl is seen to merge with all her froth and fervour into a young woman; the extravagant panegyrics of the one are tempered with the growing finesse and writing style of the other.

Six months passed when a new idol caught Barbara's eye: "... a fleeting glimpse of his profile – but so divine." And the undone Rupert was summarily refused a kiss – "because the last mouth to touch mine had been Lorenzo's." 'Lorenzo' – 'Gabriel' were Barbara's fanciful labels for the man more prosaically named Henry Harvey. Tall and handsome, affected and arrogant, Henry Harvey became a marked presence in Barbara's life. He was even purported to have an allure for both women and men. Those heady first days of tracking down 'Lorenzo' in the Bodleian, hearing his voice, his step on the stair behind her, the first invitation to the Trout, had induced in her 'that kind of gnawing at the vitals ... that is so marvellous.'

Henry's subsequent cruel teasing:- Henry 'was rude about my teeth', his sulks and silences at table, his total obduracy to commit, had only goaded her to more patience, more tolerance and ultimate hopes. Finally Barbara had tried to wean herself from her passion with small random aversions; for his long hair that badly needed cutting, his hair that had been cut too short, his fatuous smile, his new ugly navy blue hat and her crowning fury at his wrestling with her on the floor. On another amicable occasion: "he took my clothes off by sheer physical force before tea ..." but her good humour was soon restored and she ate her tea wearing "his black flannel ..." (the final sartorial detail is destroyed, along with three-quarters of the page). But Barbara's obsession for Henry Harvey had seeped back, defiantly, in waves of blissful yearning for him walking naked in the garden in Banbury Road through the summer heat wave of 1933; of her trembling all over as he stood near, by the Bibliography books. And then driving in the Bentley, she was swept back to the beginning: 'I found myself wanting to gaze all the time at Henry's divine profile, particularly those lovely hollows in his cheeks which delight me so.' And they had their moments in his rooms, in the Banbury

Road. The intimate supper parties; Barbara in her suspenders sitting on his knee and then 'Reading *Samson and Agonistes* in bed with nothing on.'

In 1934 Hilary followed Barbara to Oxford, to read Classics at Lady Margaret Hall. She cast a sisterly eye over Barbara's suitors and confirmed that Henry was attractive. She told me "he always stayed attractive and became less arrogant with age. Of course, he took himself seriously and was always about to write about somebody. At Oxford, Barbara slaved over his thesis on the 17th Century biographer and critic, Gerard Langbaine, the younger. Henry would not have coped on his own." But he became an indisputably key character – warts and all – in all Barbara's novels. Through the intervening years: his work at the British Council in Finland and Sweden, his two marriages and divorces, Henry and Barbara had corresponded with all their old affectionate banter.

3

Novel Departures

At the age of 16 years, Barbara was compelled to attempt her first novel. It was started in August 1929 and completed in April 1930. She called it *Young Men in Fancy Dress*. Never destined to be published it rests with her collection of manuscripts, note books and short stories at the Bodleian Library – "Perhaps the prize is my first novel written in 1929" she wrote to Philip Larkin in 1978, two years before her death. (The 267 pages are written in black ink with a studiously joined up hand, on cream lined paper and bound in grey cloth.)

Young Men in Fancy Dress had been inspired by Aldous Huxley's first published novel *Crome Yellow* (1921). In the early 1920's, Huxley, with his mop of silky hair, his full lips and long, lanky legs, was a cult figure. His volley of exuberant argument, sardonic wit and clever conversation cajoled his readers into a sense of their own extraordinary intelligence. Pym, never one for a wide canvas, particularly identified with Huxley's closed stage of a fine country house filled with a weekend party of young sophisticates and passés Edwardians. Huxley's *Crome Yellow* had in fact been prompted by his many visits to Garsington Manor, the home of the Lady Ottoline Morrell. With her equine nose, bony with breeding, she would sally forth into a sea of talented jeunesse dorée and sit in attentively on their boisterous debate.

Huxley's novels of the 1920's, depicting the cross fire between the 'bright young things', the posturing elitist 'souls' and the Edwardians, were read avidly. The fledgling novelists, Evelyn Waugh, Anthony Powell and Pym herself, were influenced by his inherent sense of fun and dismissive put-downs. *Young men in Fancy Dress* reflected Barbara's naïve perceptions of the 'Bohemian Set'. The richness and colour that Huxley evoked in his novels had aroused the impressionable young author and her descriptive powers.

The four-poster beds at 'Crome' he had described 'like four-masted ships, with furled sails of shining coloured stuff.' Lord David Cecil, another young protégé of Lady Ottoline, wrote of Garsington's 'Venetian-red drawing room' and her 'little sitting room upstairs book-lined and with woodwork and wainscot painted a dim peacock-green with hints of gold on the mouldings ...' and 'the hall of delicate dove-grey'. In Barbara's subsequent concoction of a Chelsea Bohemian flat, we read:

> the walls of the drawing room were a very pale green and the frieze along the top had been designed by one of Julian's artistic friends. It was very modern and carried out in shades of green, orange and brown and pale mauve that was almost grey. The curtains and cushions were of these colours and the taffeta of which they were made was shot with gold and silver.

Barbara dedicated *Young Men in Fancy Dress* to Dewi Morgan Griffith, a son she particularly admired, of the local Pastor: "who kindly informed me that I had the makings of a style of my own."

Lady Ottoline was given no quarter in Pym's novels. That tall imperious figure, bandaged in taffeta with her mauve-powdered décolletage, was no model for Pym's more modest cast of genteel women. It was the elegant Mrs Leopold Amery, wife of the distinguished politician and writer and mother of the prodigious Julian, who masqueraded in several of Pym's novels. In *Crampton Hodnet* she officiated as 'Lady Beddoes' to open a church garden party. 'But everyone agreed that it was a lovely speech. She looked so gracious, standing there in her pretty hyacinth-blue dress and her elegant hat, and her voice was so attractive, that people hardly noticed what she said.'

In July 1934, at the age of 21 years, Barbara launched herself into her first published novel – *Some Tame Gazelle*. Her story with its nucleus of Hilary and herself as spinsters projected into middle age, accompanied by a galère of friends from their Oxford circle, all similarly developed, was a curious concept; an inspired caprice, in which her mature material gave an idio-syncrasy to her script which could not have arisen with a younger cast. She wrote in her diary: "Sometime in July I began writing a story about Hilary and me as spinsters of fifty-ish. Henry, Jock and all of us appeared in it. I sent it to them – they liked it very much. So I am going on with it and one day it may become a book."

Pym's enthusiasm for her book was fuelled by the conviction that she was a natural writer; she now aspired to a quiet home life at Oswestry, setting her own literary disciplines. "I try to type 2 sides every day, and today I haven't done quite that, although on occasions I can do more," she reported on 4th October. Three days later she noted proudly: "I wrote 4 pages of my story today, and enjoyed doing it. After lunch I thought all inspiration had gone, but later it came back quite surprisingly". The most literary of her friends, Jock Liddell, sent her encouraging letters; (lifelines to Oswestry, "so awful after Oxford"). He assured her: "Henry and I think you are a very great novelist and implore you to continue your story ... Henry thinks you are far greater than Miss Austen. I don't quite agree, though I place you well above the Brontës." There had also been a comment on whether the mature 'Belinda' would have watched sister 'Harriet' – "splashing about in the bath like a plump porpoise" while quoting 'Thou art not fair for all thy red and white.' Fresh from Oxford and her absorptions with "our greater English poets", Barbara quoted liberally in *Some Tame Gazelle*. Favourite lines to soothe mild disasters were murmured across copious cups of tea. And Jock impressed on her that she had "a genius for quotation which has probably never been equalled".

Named after Thomas Haynes Bayly's lines:

Some tame gazelle, or some gentle dove
Something to love, oh, something to love!

Barbara's first novel evolved from the sisters' churchy childhood in Oswestry. (Her friend, Hazel Holt, later met at the International African Institute, had first assumed that the book was about game-hunting, with startled impala leaping out of the savannah.) Any new young curates asked to supper at Morda Lodge by their mother, would be scrutinised by the girls.

In *Some Tame Gazelle*, this scenario took on more significance, notably 'Harriet's' need to cherish and cosset the young men. Her newly baked cakes and her jellies and jam, nestling in a hand-knitted pair of socks were delivered to the curates' lodging – "something to *love*, that was the point", concluded elder sister 'Belinda'.

15

Barbara embroidered their sedate story with her inimitable props of comedy, human foibles and her wily delineations of the church and village rank. The weekly sewing lady – Miss Prior – provoked a flurry of nerves; she aspired to 'meat of some kind' for lunch. Might she be side-tracked with cauliflower cheese? The duck was for the curate's dinner. Or perhaps the curate might have the cauliflower cheese ... ' "you surely aren't suggesting that we should have the duck for lunch, are you?" asked Harriet with a note of challenge in her voice.'

The trouble was that Miss Prior was 'so very nearly a gentlewoman'. Meals in the kitchen with Emily were not an option and nor would she care to eat with Belinda and Harriet; her meals were taken in to her on a tray. But when it came to "no paper in the downstairs lavatory", Miss Prior was most confidential and far too polite to complain when handed pages from an old *Church Times.*

In *Some Tame Gazelle* Barbara portrayed an early post-war English world of manor houses, servants, cream and butter from the dairy and vegetables and strawberries from walled kitchen gardens. Any flames of romantic passion past and present – "had died down but the fire was still glowing brightly". The book was distinguished by its signal 'Pymdon', set in perpetuity.

In Oswestry, on 11th November 1935, Armistice Day, "My novel came back from being typed while I was having breakfast. They seem to have done it well and in spite of a few mistakes it looks very nice. ... I spent some time going through the novel in the evening ... I am alternately cheerful and depressed about it." On 16th November, Barbara and her mother drove to Shrewsbury where *Some Tame Gazelle* was packed off "to be in 2 volumes (in limp covers!)". They had lunch and shopped a little. "I bought a 6d lipstick. Now I'm trying to think of a plot for a new novel ..."

Some Tame Gazelle was returned on 21st November with a smart green spine and soft yellow covers. With a certain sang-froid, Barbara posted her novel to Chatto and Windus and was pleased to receive an acknowledgment three days later. As a tyro author she had no agent to advise her on a publisher. Why did she first choose Chatto? "Belles – lettres, biography and memoirs, cookery, crime and current affairs", as listed 60 years later in *The Writers' Handbook* may not have been the most appropriate depositary, but 'fiction' was included as an alternative. Two weeks later the novel was returned with an encouraging letter. Barbara made a nonchalant reference in her diary. They had found her "character drawing too detached" but her style "a pleasure to read, etc." They also thought the book too long. This cheered her; cutting and improving was a facet of her writing that she particularly enjoyed. Undaunted she sent *Some Tame Gazelle* to Gollancz; ten days later on 20th December she wrote ruefully in her diary: "Today I had two stories rejected by *London Mercury*, so that I only need my novel back from Gollancz to complete everything." The two stories were 'Unpast Alps' and 'They Never Write'. Short story writing was not Barbara's idea of fun; she even hated doing them. But home alone in Oswestry, purportedly to write, she hoped that they might be an entrée to the publishing world and precursors to her novels. "At present I am depressed," she noted on 29th December, "I want Liebe (*sic*) but I would be satisfied if my novel could be published." There was often to be this wry equation between her love life and her literary achievements. And she wrote to Jock: "Would one rather be loved by Henry or have a novel accepted?"

Some Tame Gazelle was returned from Gollancz on 2nd January 1936 "with a polite note". Barbara made no comment. It was a quiet time with her parents; meals, washing-up, shopping and good films in Shrewsbury and deferential bulletins from the wireless on the King's life coasting to a peaceful end. But Barbara was more agitated about writing a story on Budapest, and how to get hold of a typewriter and how to escape to Oxford again.

In May she sent *Some Tame Gazelle* to Macmillan; it was rejected; and by Methuen also. She set it aside and started on a new novel. Towards the end of July she could report: "I am now on the 6th chapter of my second novel, and am intending to get on with it as fast as possible . . . I'd like if possible to get the whole thing done by November. It will be something to work for . . . I can't feel it's really as good as *Some Tame Gazelle* but it may stand a better chance of getting accepted." *Adam and Cassandra* was finally completed in 1938 and destined to be published posthumously in 1987 by Macmillan. Again it revealed the considerable maturity of a girl of 23 years in her observations on human relationships. A marriage under suppression with an arrogant, bombastic husband; humoured by his adoring wife, he is finally forgiven, if not admired, by the reader. Patricia T O'Conner, an editor of

'Book Review' in *The New York Times* wrote in January 1988, a warm appraisal of the re-titled *Civil to Strangers* and its attendant selection of short stories: "Her lively and engaging world is embodied once again."

Barbara had always liked the look of Jonathan Cape's books and in July 1936 she again chanced her arm with *Some Tame Gazelle*. On 14th August she received a heartening letter from Jonathan Cape himself. He was interested in her novel and if she could make certain alterations he might even be able to publish it. She confided to her diary: "I dare not hope too much, but it would be marvellous if he took it." She wondered why Cape would want to publish *Some Tame Gazelle* when Macmillan et al did not. Writing to Henry at Oxford she confessed she would cry if Cape did not take it. She worked on the few minor alterations and returned the typescript with cautious expectations. (Jock Liddell had described Jonathan Cape to her as "a square grey man and he is very kind but rather bleak".) The novel was returned to her in September with expressed regrets: wrote Jonathan Cape: "There is not here the unanimity of appreciation of the book's chances that I feel is essential for successful publication. Personally I like your novel, but I fear that if I were to offer to publish it, we would be unable to give it all the care and attention which I feel are necessary if it is be successfully launched."

A bitter blow for Barbara and a portent of the annihilating rejection that she eventually would suffer from Cape in the early 1960's. There were tears, but no recriminations. Two years later she approached Cape for a job in publishing. There was no work for her but Jonathan Cape remembered her novel; he urged her to keep writing. It was in 1945, as she tended her dying mother at Oswestry, that Barbara checked through *Some Tame Gazelle* for alterations and immaturities. Luckily for her it had not become dated by the passing decade. The English pre-war beneficent life was still comfortably reflected in country villages. She sent her revised version to Cape in February 1949. This time it was accepted. Liddell wrote to her, joyfully: "I know the burden that is lifted off one, when at last the reproach of one's barrenness is done away."

Published in May 1950, it was well received with substantial reviews. Wrote Pamela Hansford Johnson in *The Daily Telegraph*: "Miss Pym's sharp fresh fun is all her own. There is also an amiable air of scholarship about this novel which I find most pleasing." Antonia White in the *New Statesman* professed that Pym worked in 'petit point' and made each stitch with 'perfect precision'. The more seasoned Anatole Broyard wrote:

"The usual remark made about Barbara Pym is that she is Jane Austen recreated, but ... she is funnier and she works more on the fringes of society. Her heroines are characterised by an irrepressible honesty." Michael Gorra, the freelance critic, wrote a perceptive review for the novel's second edition in *The New York Times*, 31st July 1983, under "Restraint is the point": "Almost everything in *Some Tame Gazelle* takes place across a middle-class table. But Miss Pym's world is one of chaos barely reduced in order; her work is not as complacent as the surfaces of the scenes she describes." Gorra conceded that the then 37-year-old author, with her insight on secret pain and vulnerability had brought the two sisters to self-recognition; 'Belinda' to admit that her unrequited love for pompous Henry was at worst 'pathetic', but it was necessary. 'Harriet's' giddy pampering of fresh young curates was shown to give "substance to an otherwise shadowy existence". Gorra could find no rough, immature edges, characteristic of a first novel. "*Some Tame Gazelle* is a completely controlled and realised consideration of the themes to which this unusually consistent writer returned in her nine succeeding novels." A conclusion which Larkin later promulgated in his article on Pym for the *Times Literary Supplement* (1977): "... as novels they exhibit no 'development'; the first is as practised as the last, the observation, the social comedy, the interplay of themes equally expert."

4

Gorgeous Gordon

Few writers with the slender compilation of twelve novels can have been so assiduously analysed as Barbara Pym. A dyed in the wool Anglican? An anthropologist? An academic manqué? A comic? She could even be judged a potential psychoanalyst with her acute observations of the social order from her own quiet parameters.

A clever, attractive single woman, with an abundance of humour and charm, irresistibly begs the question: was she sexy? From the intimations of her diary we find no frank sexual revelations. But her yearnings from unrequited love should not be underestimated: "My love for 'Gabriel' has been by no means all honey – in fact no honey at all ..." she wrote in her vacation. Instead we read the signal outpourings of an infatuated woman, of a woman in love and the gruelling anguish of a woman spurned. Pym's most enduring clue to her sensuality could yet be her girlish reference to 'that kind of gnawing at the vitals sick feeling .... that is so marvellous.'

Henry Harvey, despite his peripatetic attentions must rank as Pym's lifelong love, correspondent and friend. He hinted at her sexual libido in a talk at the Pen Club in October 1985. He portrayed her, in her Oxford hey-day, as a flirtatious extrovert, out to track the man of her particular fancy. But there the playing had to stop. "Barbara was no houri," affirmed Harvey. "Being in love was pretend play. She was without sensuality ... her passions," he assured his rapt audience, "stayed in her head and heart." The trackings down, the yearnings and the romantic plots were strangely dissipated when the prey was ensnared, to be candidly re-created in her writings; as an icon objective of romantic beauty perhaps, lovingly stuffed for posterity.

Harvey's predilection for his fellow graduate, the writer Robert Liddell, was an added challenge to Pym. She befriended the diminutive, 'pretty'

Liddell, as a confidant. They complained happily about Harvey together, he sitting demurely with his small hands clasped in his lap, crossing his legs at the ankles, whilst she shared the cooking in their lodgings and darned their idol's socks. Pym and Liddell were to become the most indulgent of correspondents, freely airing their fears and frustrations. It was "Dear Pym" or "Dear Pymska" and even "My Dear Cassandra Pym" in the first years of her fledgling novels. It was to Liddell that Pym poured out her shock over her mother's 'bad motor accident' in January 1936. Driving over a country crossroad a motorcycle "hit us a tremendous smack and sent the car up into a hedge." Two boys lay motionless in the road. "They were both bleeding horribly and it was a dreadful sight ..." The ambulance finally came ... "we just stood about and couldn't do anything for the poor boys. They both had fractured skulls and one died almost as soon as he got to the infirmary. Our car is very badly smashed ..."

A year later in February 1937 Liddell was complaining to her: "I write from a bed of sickness, viz. a cold caught in the Bodleian Library." A few days later: "As I still have a cold there is really no place like bed, and I quite wonder why people with nothing to prevent them do not usually spend the months of February there." By April he could report gastric trouble and a toothache. "Thank you for your letter – it was a comfort to me. I hope you will soon write again for I may be in greater need of comfort." He finally sent the more cheering news that he hoped to be spending the summer more peacefully in a nursing home, "because it is possible that I have appendicitis. I have seen three doctors who were divided in their opinions ..."

Harvey tried to jolly Liddell along, from his own more settled and happy life in Helsingfors. In his small scrawl he tried to engage Liddell's mind on melons. He wrote in October 1937: "My dear Jock, would you believe it, but Finland in the summer, produces the most delicious melons, and, firm and sweet, they have lasted longer this year and we have been eating them every day. They are grown out of doors. This is the first convincing proof I have had that Finland is really hot in the summer." Mindful perhaps of his friend's chronic health anxieties, he ended on an intuitive note: "In spite of them I am afraid my stomach has been bad."

Pym kept Liddell's subsequent letters from Egypt and Greece, intact in their envelopes, which were adorned with ravishing stamps. Classical statues,

Queen's heads clasped in pearl circlets, naked youths wrestling with dragons, palaces, newly designed airplanes and fairly-tale monasteries perched high on sheer cliffsides above swirling seas, all arrest the eye. Pym's loyal correspondent, fastidious in all his tastes, would have chosen each stamp with inordinate care and pleasure. Meanwhile Pym clung to her stalking format, of tracking Harvey to the Bodleian, to Blackwell's, to Elliston's restaurant and even past his digs in the Banbury Road to gaze up at his lighted bedroom window. Harvey persistently asked her to tea but Pym, as persistently, refused. The thrill of the unknown, bolstered by her own imaginings of love's delicious rapture, was not so soon to be levelled by reality.

In tandem with Pym's perception of romantic love relationships was her absorption with the platonic. Although she could be intoxicated by a man's handsome profile, it was his heart and mind and sanction that she hankered after. The idea of the sexual act was to become a 'pis aller', a final denigration of the original passion. In her middle years it was the walks and talks with professors and poets and the younger homosexuals, where she felt most comfortable. Having wryly forecast spinsterhood at the age of 25 years, Pym undoubtedly felt a certain sadness that she never married. She appeared to have more empathy with cats than children. Her life was structured and disciplined to her own tune and with a discreet assortment of male escorts (heading for their booksy consignments) she kept herself employed. Her closer friends gave her the opportunity to observe the underlying strains of marriage and divorce. In her early forties she noted tauntingly in her diary: "with the years men get more bumbling and vague, but women get sharper." Although divorce per se is not a storyline in her novels, her mild chronicling of a marital combat can cut to the core. To the end of her life, it was 'being in love' and its attendant exhilarations that Pym craved. Both her failed and her fulfilling pursuits were invariably transmitted to a novel. The comeuppance and the deliverance of her amalgamated heroines and heroes would embellish the tale.

It was Gordon Glover, writer for *The Radio Times* and broadcaster, with whom Barbara fell giddily in love. They met in December 1941 when he was amicably entailed in divorce proceedings. His wife, Honor, had taken a house in Clifton, a pretty suburb of Bristol, where she lived with their children. Pym, assigned to the censorship office at Bristol and Hilary, working with the BBC Schools' Department, had joined Honor at The Coppice. Shortly before her death in 1998, Honor Wyatt Ellidge reminisced on the youthful Pym sisters, in a talk to the Barbara Pym Society. They had both always possessed 'the secret of youth'. Barbara, tall and well-dressed with a certain reserve and Hilary, less reflective and vivacious. They would talk earnestly together about clothes, never going to bed without the next day's outfit meticulously put out at the ready. Their voices were particularly distinctive and rang through the house. "Keeping four people in toilet rolls seemed rather a burden." Barbara's plummy tones made Honor and her children laugh. Long after her friend died, Honor could hear Pym's voice 'persist in the head' as she read her passages of dialogue, to bring it magically alive. The glib and glamorous Glover descended regularly on this nest of women to visit his children. Writing to Harvey in October 1942, Pym described her new friend. She claimed that Gordon Glover reminded her of him ... 'A great philanderer but very sweet and kind and as I haven't fallen in love with him I see only his best side. So strange being reminded of you – I didn't think anyone ever could do that.' Debonair and conventionally handsome Glover proved a bewitching companion, with a facile command of anecdote and literary 'bons mots'. Hilary who was prone to less sanguine opinions of Pym's heartthrobs described Glover to me as 'raffish, smug and smart'.

By November 1942, Glover had declared his ill-fated love, which Pym soon confessed had pitched her into 'this great chunk of misery'. The crux of their passionate tumble had been sustained for a mere two months. Moonlight and kisses on the Suspension Bridge, evening strolls in churchyards, enlivened by spotted flycatchers, snatched visits to London... Honor's own deep absorption with the writer, George Ellidge, whom she later married, gave a salutary blessing to the whole affair. On the verge of her divorce from Glover, Honor, sensed Pym's extreme vulnerability and later regretted not warning her of Glover's devilish and facile attentions. But what if his love had been serious? She chose not to interfere or caution or to spoil matters. Then he telephoned ... a letter from Pym had "expressed expectations" ... and Honor had the anguish of exposing her husband's bluff to her closest friend.

Thirty three years after their liaison, Pym was constrained to admit that she had been only a passing infatuation and burned her diary entries for 1942. In the following year she noted and agonised over Glover's cavalier exit: 'it's a slow wrenching away, painful at once, afterwards just sad and dreary.' She later wrote to Harvey that it took her a full nine months to recover – '(just like having a baby)'. But Pym had a staying power with her lovers; after the war, Glover, remarried to a former girlfriend, took Pym out to a long lunch in London: 'Pagani's – Lobster', she recorded tersely. Her love and yearning for Glover – 'with his hair smoothed down sitting opposite me at breakfast in The Coppice kitchen on a Monday morning' – had finally subsided.

For all his wounding unreliability, Glover was a natural candidate for Pym's two bestselling novels. His flirtatious wit and charm was revived in "Rockingham Napier", the naval lieutenant, from her flagship comedy *Excellent Women*. When the mousy Mildred Lathbury opened her door, she was transfixed by his beguiling manner and his handsome dark looks. She offered him coffee and within five minutes the conversation had embraced Aubrey Beardsley, High Mass and acolytes and English gentlewomen in Italy with Baedekers. Mildred felt rather dazed when he turned his smile full on her. She also found his dislike of having anything to do with Church before breakfast a little frivolous. "Rocky Napier" was the perfect panacea to exonerate Pym's love and pain.

Glover must have been gratified to see himself resurrected yet again in Pym's third novel *Jane and Prudence*. This time he was less indulgently portrayed as "Fabian Driver" the smooth, serial womaniser who dwelt so little on his wife's existence that her death was a shock to him. His subsequent target was "Prudence", with whom Pym particularly identified: 'Prudence Bates was twenty-nine, an age that is often rather desperate for a woman who has not yet married.' "Fabian Driver" unnerved her with his penetrating glance. She distrusted good-looking men. Theatres and dinners had ensued. But "Fabian's" spoiling attentions soon waned. Was he over-preoccupied with the Parochial Church Council, wondered the ingenuous "Prudence"? But it was another shrewder lady who had taken "Fabian" away from her; and with that characteristic hand to the brow he had finally relinquished his despairing hold of "Prudence" ... ' "one has had to hurt people, I suppose," said "Fabian", tilting his head to one side. He had just realized that the distinguished-looking man sitting at that distant table was himself reflected in a mirror at the far end of the room.'

In a treatise on Pym's work, written summer 1993 for the *Anglican Theological Review,* the dominant agreed theme to evolve was love; love in all its dimensions and permutations.

"For Pym romantic love is the most totally encompassing form of love and therefore the most important ..." words written by a graduate student at Northwestern University, USA, rejoicing in the name, Belinda Bede. A coincidence indeed to be named after Pym's timid heroine in her first novel *Some Tame Gazelle.* Bede also cited unpredictability in Pym's romantic equations; but warns that the length and depth of a sudden romance cannot be judged. It is true that in some instances, Pym's characters can veer from an instant dislike to inexplicable captivation. In the unpredictability of things, Pym performs a master touch. And the alternative of initiating a new swain or lady to the closing pages of a story could have proved arduous.

An Anglican? We see no evidence in Pym's diaries or novels that she was a scrupulously devout person. Her mild attitudes and aspirations were more honed to a kind and gentle community spirit. Church-going was a good habit devolved from her childhood. And the perfunctory prayer on the first page of *A Glass of Blessings.* – "I closed my eyes and prayed for myself, on this my thirty third birthday, for my husband Rodney, my mother-in-law Sybil and a vague collection of friends who always seemed to need praying for" – openly reflects, in her favourite heroine, Wilmet Forsyth, a healthy disrespect for pious sentiment. It was church activity, that integral axis for the village body, that point of reference for good English middle class tradition that seized her pen. The warring factions of the volunteer and the curmudgeon; the church rota with its precedence of 'excellent women' assigned to the care of the altar brasses, to the altar flowers or to 'just filling vases with water from the tap outside'. As Pym's characters stumble through pain and pleasure, she 'steers' them, in their romances and renunciations to the perception of hope and change and a personal freedom. It could be mooted that Pym strayed over to humanism with her optimistic belief in the plenipotential of the ordinary being. She especially revered the vulnerable and the failed as estimable souls. With her rooted capacity to love romantically and above all compassionately, she had her faith in the primal good overcoming evil.

Another of her close friends contributing to the Pen Club talk in October 1985, was Professor Robert Smith. They went on regular church crawls in

London and often lunched. Smith made the point that her churchy chapters – however serious – were never solemn. The clergy unanimously appreciated her meticulous research and detail. Such matters as the correct choice of altar cloths, the vestment to be worn on Mid-Lent-Sunday, the dates of the church year … all reflected Pym's respect for accuracy.

5

Encounters Encore

The downturn of Barbara's romances and travels transposed her angst into her writing. By 1935 she already had her first two novels – *Some Tame Gazelle* and *Civil to Strangers* – well in hand. The war was to prove another spur to short stories and a radio play – *Something to Remember*. Writing had become Barbara's raison d'être. She had confessed to her diary in 1936, on her summer vacation at Oswestry: 'I must *work* at my novel, that is the only thing there is and the only way to find any happiness at present.'

Rupert, Harry, Henry, Friedbert, Anton, Hanns ... . (And here we are reminded of Barbara's heroine, Prudence, in *Jane and Prudence*: 'Laurence and Henry and Philip, so many of them for she had had numerous admirers, all coming up the drive, in a great body, it seemed, though in fact they had come singly.) And in December 1937, like a meteor from some alien sphere, there was Jay. He had spotted her in Oxford, lunching with a fellow old Etonian, Denis Pullein-Thompson. Barbara in exuberant vein had been airing her Finnish and was introduced as Päävikki Olafsson. The young man with his smooth dark hair promptly inveigled Barbara back to his rooms in Balliol. He plied her with German and Hungarian records. At Barbara's height and six years younger he was astonishingly sophisticated and reported to be brilliant. She was surprised when he led her to a sofa, took her hand and kissed her. The age differential which attracted her the most as she grew older, was to open up a whole new motif in her novels.

Hilary, who met Jay at Oxford, the following year, was not so enamoured, dismissing him as, 'a funny little thing, but rather fascinating'. The younger son of Leo Amery, the Churchillian politician, Jay was himself determined on some remarkable career. A young man in a hurry, his diplomatic dreams were soon to land him in the Balkans and the Middle East. Barbara, enchanted with Julian's attentions so soon after Henry's vexing exit, sat back and enjoyed the ride – 'I feel very Hungarian' he wrote to her in January 1938, from Oxford. 'Write to me and tell me what you're doing and thinking, and don't forget to tell me when you're coming.' He gave her lunch in Balliol; chicken, and chocolate mousse and Niersteiner; there were kisses under a tree in the Botanical Gardens, a bunch of violets and a spray of mauve orchids. Barbara wrote him 'Betjeman' verses:

And I took a glass used before.
And filled it to the brim
And I thought as I drank of the night before
When I had been with him . . .

This was rewarded with more lunch in Balliol 'we had fish, duck and green peas, peaches and cream, sherry, Niersteiner and port.' (Their haphazard post prandial on the sofa was summarily interrupted by Woodrow Wyatt, then editor of *The Oxford Comment*). Their confidences exchanged and respective dreams were heightened perhaps by Julian's Hungarian melancholy. (Hungarians are professed to celebrate crying). His paternal grandmother had been Hungarian; hustled out of the country with the abortive revolution of 1848 she was brought to London. The impulsive attraction between Julian and Barbara had been more a show of romance; a mannered caprice; a dialogue of minds. With a final flourish of two dozen daffodils and an endearing card in German, Julian stepped out of her life. In March 1938, he had left for Spain as a war correspondent, to report on Franco. Barbara noted in her diary that in the space of three months, they had spent a mere twenty hours together. She later conceded that those hours had left her with 'twenty years of memories'.

In August 1938, Barbara took up a teaching position with a family in Katowice; an industrial town in flat country, some 50 miles west of Krakow. On leaving Oxford, she had felt the need to stretch her initiative and . . . to work. She taught English to the mother and daughters Ula and Zuza, the family of Dr Alberg. Especially strange sightings were jotted in her diary: "a wolf's carcase hanging outside a food shop; peasants barefooted in dark romantic forests; prostitutes swept up and taken away in a horse-drawn van; fried potatoes served with yoghurt and an exotic church of 'turquoise marble, pink, grey, dark grey, white fawn, green crochet work around the pulpit and altars in green and puce." In her mackintosh and shabby Austrian hat, Barbara walked eagerly with the Albergs, up mountains and through lovely princely gardens. Unaware of the mounting portents of war between Germany and England, Barbara was surprised and hugely disappointed to be summarily packed off home. Her aspirations had been admirable but her judgement had soon proved calamitous. The Albergs being Jewish were under no illusion of the dangers afoot.

A year later Barbara chanced on Julian in Portman Square. He took her off to 112 Eaton Square – on the sunny north side – to meet his mother. A forceful lady with blood stemming from the American Revolution, she was ambitious for her son. Barbara, sensing good copy from this last private house in the Square was sharply observant. She relished the wafts of incense and Turkish cigarettes, and the clutch of shooting sticks by the front door; the oil paintings and faded sepia family photographs of travels and distinguished service did not escape her. The view of the trees across the Square was etched on her mind, together with the notion that Mrs Leo Amery would make 'a splendid character for a novel'. A formidable political hostess, she and Julian were soon propelled into Barbara's short war stories and novels. Later masquerades evolved, of the elegant mother and her son, the admired fledgling politician; or of the diplomat's wife with a propensity to drop bricks; her embarrassed son alongside, so poised, so ineluctably perfect.

From the Pym archives in the Bodleian Library we have a sonnet written 'To a Dear Young Friend on the Third Day of December Nineteen Thirty Eight, it being the First Anniversary of our Meeting.'

My melancholy disembodied Fingers
Caress the letters and the Faded Flowers
My Gothick spirit obstinately lingers
In long-forgotten Places, Haunts of ours

Where we loved in a proctorial* way
Did twine our hands and for a moment stay
We were those lovers parted in the Spring
Who never met upon this Earth again
Yet on the Last Day when the Dead shall rise
And bones be clothed with flesh, this dusty thing
Our love that in so long a sleep has lain,
Shall spring to life in our new-fashioned Eyes,
Then shall Belgravia and North Oxford see
The Decorous Kiss of Immortality.

3rd December 1938

Barbara never met Julian Amery again but followed his career keenly. His eminent war record and his political achievements, to culminate as Minister of Aviation 1962–4, were to surpass all the old dreams and imagining of 1938. On learning in 1942 that Julian had become a Major in the Persian Army, Barbara was amused and delighted. She hope that the 'Persian Major' would wear a fez – 'dark red, preferably'. But Barbara's long term fond curiosity was doomed. The trajectory of Julian's life set them worlds apart. (At the last he was to be totally unco-operative over her biography.)

Barbara's infatuation with Julian still gushed through her mind in the 1940's. Had she loved him in that happy spring of two years ago? To love a man, younger than oneself was absurd and intoxicating – 'Everybody should try it – no life can be complete without it,' she avowed to her diary. And with a hint of Schadenfreude, she wrote one of her best stories – Goodbye Balkan Capital – gleaned from news soundings of Julian's progress through Bulgaria and the Middle East.

In her early fifties she was to be introduced to a rich and rugged young Bahamian and a more enduring relationship. With his diplomatic family connections in Nassau he would fascinate Barbara with evocative talk of a black butler and peacocks. 'His life there is full of such rich material for fiction, but I suppose it is really beyond my range.' She was writing to her old friend, Bob Smith, the historian and Africanist who had effected the

* Some versions have 'poetical'.

32

introduction. Instead she absorbed herself with the London world of antiques, the world of Richard Roberts; and more especially with his charm and quintessential youth. She drew on their romantic friendship for her novel – *The Sweet Dove Died*; an intuitive response to the constraints of a woman's desires for a younger man of variable sexual appetite.

6

The Wrennish Façade

Pym's anguish over the feckless Glover virtually catapulted her into the WRNS. Her two years of service life from July 1943 was a clean break with all associations of their bruising love affair. She took care to hide her initial sense of detachment and irony towards service life. She felt a fake. "My Wrennish façade," she wrote in her diary. She felt out of place. At the Nore Training Depot at Rochester, she was thrown into the rigours of her first pro-Wren squad drills. What was she doing there? Who were all these disparate women? It all seemed absurd.

She looked back nostalgically to those early war days at Oswestry Military Camp. At the YMCA canteen, she had busily poached eggs in little machines, been called "a wee smasher" by a Scotsman, and had lovingly varnished her nails with 'pink clover'. She had even yearned momentarily after "a ravishingly handsome second lieutenant" who, to her chagrin, was intent only on studying his book on Gas Drill. And there had been the 'Baby Clinic'. She was proud to learn to feed them and pick them up "with a nonchalant air". Then First Aid – and all those long lectures. How she had despaired of the 'circulation of the blood'. There was a night rota for the First Aid post and a supply of scratchy Army blankets. Pym's war novels, set in Oswestry, were written virtually on the hoof. *Home Front Novel* and her spy novel *So Very Secret* were both to be published posthumously. When she was not jotting down facts and vivid impressions Pym found time to read. In the winter months of 1941, she had set about "improving my mind": Austen's *Emma* – Johnson's *Tour in the Hebrides* with Boswell – *Vanity Fair* and in a rare tranquil moment, she sat drying her hair by the kitchen fire, curled up in a basket chair with the cat, and reading *To the Lighthouse* by Virginia Woolf.

And there were flirtations: Desmond with his slicked-back hair and

Stewart, a Scottish gunner. He and Pym when out to tea, to the pictures, ate ice cream and held hands. She had been taught some Gaelic. Such childish comforts had been light relief from the onerous round of duties.

At Morda House, Irena Pym, her two daughters and her one maid, Dilys, faced a mounting pressure of household jobs. They soon had five children and their mothers billeted on them from the Birkenhead shipyard district; bed-wetting, head lice, noisy, rampaging scally-wags and homesick mothers exacerbated the daily round. The blackout needed obsessive patching on Morda Lodge's large and copious windows; clothes and sheets were continuously re-cycled and washed by hand; the bed making and a compulsive attention to food, lurked like a predatory menace throughout the day. As did the gas masks, hung up with their accusing snouts, waiting to be practised with – while making the beds or hoovering with the one vacuum cleaner. The sisters shopped, queuing in damp, depressing mornings, facing shortages of such mundane necessities as torch batteries, matches and any normal comforts such as cigarettes and drink. Food, or a lack of it was always at the front of their minds. Pym recorded any stray treats in her diary: "supper of curried eggs, fried eggs and potatoes – and felt really full." At her aunt's house, she had drooled over "tomato sandwiches, blackberry jam – scones and bread, Swiss roll and chocolate cake". With the lawns and borders at Morda Lodge dug up for vegetables and soft fruit, there could never have been any intractable food crisis. Despite the chains of duty, Pym had not been deterred from her writing: "After supper I did some more 'writing' – which quells my restlessness – that is how I must succeed!" Pym had been confident on 'The Home Front', in her hometown; one of a team. Although enemy planes had passed over at night to target Liverpool, life had been relatively peaceful in Oswestry. She had felt needed and secure in her place. In 1941, her restless urge to do something more, to work away from home, was answered by an edict from the Ministry of Labour. All unmarried women between 19 and 30 years were to register for war work …

Forming up in line with the Wrens was no place for nostalgia. Pym braced herself. Squad drill standing to attention, learning to salute, was worlds away from the cosy green pastures of the Oswestry YMCA canteen. It was an accepted fact that the WRNS was the most popular of the Women's Services. Volunteers were drawn inexorably to its aura of naval glamour. Pym had never been class conscious; it was the cultural rapport that she craved. "I don't think there are really any of our kind of people, though there are one or two pleasant ones." On a scorching hot afternoon, she went on a four-mile route march. They passed a fine 18th Century church in a churchyard of long waving grass and an urn tomb. It was such observations that nourished her during the bewildering first weeks as a trainee. She described tug trips in drenching rough seas; climbing up 'scarifying' boat ladders and how volunteers were lowered in a rope sling from an upper window. "I couldn't have done it – it made me quite sick to look at it." And the grim refrain "doggedly to bed" ran through her diary, and still she ached for Glover: "... the thought of Gordon ... a longing, a regret, a sadness ..." She wanted him – he was "a raw wound" in her mind.

The novelty of being a Wren was wearing off. She missed music and talk and companionship. She had sometimes managed to hear music pro-grammes on the Foc'sle wireless. At Smith's she had picked up a copy of *Tristram Shandy* and a Graham Greene novel, which she later devoured in the afternoons on her bunk. A copy of the *Radio Times* made luxurious reading. After supper she would sometimes walk or bicycle with her friends Prue Leith Ross and Joyce Gresham, to Southend: "It is definitely a common place with no charm as far as I can see – one great street of shops – Woolworths, Marks and Spencer and cheap stores – pin-tables and amusement halls – cinemas – the whole place smelling of fish and chips – raffish – and an enormous hotel, the Palace." But Southend had its moments, with its Odeon cinema, the occasional concert and the Women's Services Club; a convenience of refreshment rooms and a library. At her new job in 'Regulating Office' she was given her own single cabin and could smoke, and drink as much tea as she wished. She was pleased with her new haircut, set in pageboy style. Gradually the break from back home was eased and fun and camaraderie opened out. "It has given me confidence," she admitted to herself after her first two months in service. One summer evening, she and Joyce explored the Palace; a vast smoky dance hall cram-med with soldiers and cadets, Poles and Americans. They bought themselves "harmless little half pints" and got talking with a couple of cadets. They were asked to dance. "I'm trying to see the funny side," Pym reminded herself. She and Joyce conceded that "It was quite an enjoyable, queer kind of evening – and I know I should love it if I had someone nice (and tall) to dance with."

Pym got her Commission; by March 1944 she was a Third Officer in the Southampton Censorship office and could only draw praise from her Directors. She had been judged 'intelligent and adaptable' and took 'a keen interest' in her work. She now wrote more enthusiastically of her life, to Harvey, stationed in Stockholm. She was agreeably situated at Exbury House, eighteen miles from Southampton and close to the Solent shore. With Lionel de Rothschild's death in 1942, the grand neo-classic mansion had been occupied by the Admiralty – "A large country house with beautiful grounds full of camellias, azaleas and rhododendrons," she reported. She was also intrigued that successive generations of the Mitford family had lived in the Exbury 'School House'. It was Lionel de Rothschild who had bought the estate in 1918 and had transformed an area of rough woodland and poor soil into the rare and renowned gardens of today. "Am now more or less heart free," she continued to Harvey. She had met some nice Army captains – one had even been up at Magdalen 1936–1939. She had enjoyed an Anglo/American dance at the Village Hall. They had worn civilian clothes; her officer's uniform was stiff and uncomfortable for dancing but she had found it much smarter than her 'wrens'. "... it is made to measure and fits much better; gold buttons and a tricorne hat with a rather beautiful naval badge, blue and gold and crimson."

She asked Harvey how he looked. Had he still got all his hair? She ended: "I am vaguely depressed, waiting for things to happen as we all are now. I wish it could be over and done with – we shall know so many people in it and I suppose a good many of them won't come back. Still, I wouldn't be anywhere else now at this time." Meanwhile social life in Southampton, under the aegis of the English and American invasion forces, was pitched to a fast pace. The abundant ratio of men to women put the Wrens at a high premium. Pym and her fellow officers were swamped with invitations.

In September 1944 Pym was posted to Naples, a comparatively calm base, between the fighting in the north of Italy and naval action in the Mediterranean. Social life again blazed through the port, with dances held in grand occupied villas or on board ship. Couples swayed languorously on the quarterdeck beside the moonlit bay, to a band of the Royal Marines. Pym best enjoyed the wind and spray in the motorboat trip back to shore. In her diary she described her day at Axel Munthe's villa in Anacapri; she found it evocative with rooms crammed with elegant old furniture and local sculpture. In the garden she was drawn to "a cool little courtyard full of these Roman pieces, white walled and peaceful with trees against the sky. I felt tears coming into my eyes and had to turn away. The peace, the beauty, the antiquity, perhaps something of the feeling I have for churchyards came over me." Further along she found a corner high up above the sea with a marble bench, sheltered by towering cypresses. A stone harpy was silhouetted against the sky and sea. But Pym found life in the Censorship Division with the va et vient of staff at the Naples Base strangely dull and unrewarding. However she hugely valued the trips with Army officers to Ischia, Positano, Ravello and Amalfi. She also made time to write up her diaries and notebooks. Those scenic vistas of cypresses and olives, lemon and orange groves, Byzantine churches and "rich idle Italians playing cards all night ..." were rare vignettes to be re-invented for her future novels. In 1963, 20 years on, we read of 'Ianthe Broome' in *An Unsuitable Attachment* stepping out on to her little rickety looking balcony and gazing down "over acres of lemon groves ... Ianthe could feel that there were hundreds, perhaps thousands, of lemons hanging there among the leaves."

Pym now took an invidious pleasure in recording her boredom. "Boredom is an exquisite experience," she recalled of one night that she and her friend, Margaret, had gone out with 'Pete'. The two girls had taken it in turns to shuffle round the floor with him at the 'Orange Grove'. "Conversation with Pete is an impossibility." Matters had improved with 'Captain Heaven', Jimmy, at the 22 Club where they swam and sunbathed. In the evening he had taken her to the opera house – The Teatro San Carlo – to hear Grieg's Piano Concerto. Pym had found the auditorium "luscious" in its baroque exuberance, with tiered red plush and gold boxes and painted ceiling. Her diary entry was transmitted thirty years later to her novel *The Sweet Dove Died*, when that impressionable ambience was evoked for Leonora's evening out at Covent Garden. Pym's attitude to her social life and her work became more despondent. Despite censoring up to two hundred letters a day, she felt unfulfilled, undervalued, and thoroughly satiated with parties and drinks with "too many drunken majors".

Her friend Jimmy warned her that she had been referred to as "that very blasé Wren officer with a perpetually bored expression". However, her friend Cynthia passed on an encouraging quote: "The girl with the fascinating eyes." At the peak of her truculence, Pym struck lucky. A tall, dark, dashing lieutenant, secretary to the Chief of Staff, talking vivaciously at the centre of a group, caught her eye. 'Starky' as she was to call him, intrigued and provoked her. It seemed to her that it was the first time in Naples that she had shared a good conversation. As they hung over the balcony above the bay they talked about everything and nothing and, notably, "About Sex!" Starky's penetrating brown eyes, his nonchalance and cynicism and his basic "commonness" and bad accent all connived to make her wildly attracted to him. "I hope you will not throw yourself away," wrote the fastidious Liddell from Egypt. She had written of her irresistibly "handsome beast" who had intelligence but no culture. In Liddell's eyes, Pym was the perennial Anglo–Catholic, with her emotions and her singular life well in control. (He was subsequently indignant over the publication of *A Very Private Eye*; it had exposed her youthful "flighty" years and "cheapened her image".) Pym's infatuation for Starky added flavour to life. He was casual and rude and articulate. Pym emphasised in her diary that their relationship was physical rather than cultural. Dinners at the British Officer's Club, at the Fleet Club; dancing at the Churchill, the Orange Grove, the 22 Club, the US Naval Dance, the RAF Dance. Starky soon suspected she was in love with him because she called him "darling" – "... but you say it so many times". Once again, Pym had lavished love from her head and her heart; noticing that Starky was unpopular with his peers, had made her feelings "fiercely protective". It is unlikely that her full-bloodied consort had sought sex with such a superior and raffiné woman. In Pym's fashion any physical equation would have stopped short with her preferred "gnawing at the vitals".

After this sybaritic interlude it was a shock to Pym to hear that Starky was poised to return to England. She agonised to herself and then to her friend, Morag, who said she was wallowing in emotion. Pym liked to wallow in emotion and confided to herself – "... does one <u>ever</u> learn not to mind!" She and Starky spent a happy last day together climbing up Vesuvius – through pretty woods with views over the Bay and a long plod upwards through the ash and lava. According to Pym's account Starky was unusually attentive and carried her hat and bag. They peered into the crater hand in hand. Their descent was hysterical with Pym laughing uncontrollably, repeatedly falling down in the warm ash and grazing her legs. It is to be hoped that her hat and bag survived. A few days later, Starky left early by plane. Pym was writing to him within two days. She described her letter as "quite a good one which will no doubt be beyond him". He replied once, signing himself 'Iain'. Three weeks later Pym was still on daily visits to sickbay; a throbbing blister on her heel needed constant dressing; the aftermath of their happy last day. "Thanks for a lovely volcano," she had gulped when they finally had parted at 3 am. Still, "Why doesn't Starky write?" She fretted and then in more sanguine vein: "But how quickly I forget those bright brown eyes, that sweet smile, that uncertain gauche social manner . . ." and in her inimitable custom, Pym re-invented 'Starky' twenty years on as the unsuitable suitor for 'Ianthe' in *An Unsuitable Attachment*. 'John Challow' – tall, dark, young, handsome with slightly disturbing brown eyes tired 'Ianthe' with his over talkative manner. She also noticed that "his shoes seemed a little too pointed. . ."

In March 1945, Pym and her party drove up by Cassino; gutted and flattened, the surrounding villages were in ruins with "sightless windows". But the countryside on the way to Rome was ravishing. Her eye was sharp and re-invigorated by the enforced gap in her writing. "Country lovely – brilliant green grass, yellow-green trees, blossoms and cypresses as one gets further north – villages on hills grey with a church spire or cupola . . ." In Rome she marvelled at St Peter's vastness, the rich and varied marble decoration and the buttery yellow Siena marble. From the roof they saw the palazzo Venezia with its flying roof statues and everywhere campanili, pinnacled domes and towers, marked the blazing sky. Pym reported the Tiber "a yellowish brown" and to her delight, in bizarre contrast to the panoramic grandeur, spread far below, she found "hens on the roof". It was Palm Sunday and she and a girlfriend were to lunch at the Officers' Club in Pincio Gardens, adjoining Villa Borghese. There is a photograph of them, seated at a table on the balcony. Glamorous with shoulder length hair and in uniform, they are gazing intently at the handsome young officer placed between them.

Pym returned home on May 31st, on compassionate leave. Her mother was dying of abdominal cancer. She spent the summer "hanging around" at the WRNS Headquarters in Queen's Gate, alternated with increasingly sad and anxious visits to Oswestry. It was a miserable time for the two daughters; their mother died on September 10th. Irena's zest and energy and her unusual foresight in bypassing the Oswestry day school for a more challenging education had propelled her two girls on their rewarding careers. Pym and Hilary were pleased to get back to London, and set up a new life together in a modest flat, on the second floor of a house in Pimlico: "... so very much the 'wrong' side of Victoria Station, so definitely *not* Belgravia," said 'Mildred', disparagingly, in *Excellent Women*.

7

Pym's Post War London

108 Cambridge Street was a solid Victorian corner house with a glazed first floor sun balcony. Pym's spacious bedroom gave directly on St Gabriel's Church in Warwick Square. A secluded ambience still envelops this quiet corner with ash trees and maples and the soaring branches of the square beyond. The cream pillared and stuccoed terraces stretch away in bland respectability. Pym wrote to Harvey that she was delighted with their new flat and London civilian life. They had acquired a lot of pieces from Oswestry, their father having given up his house to live in the Wynnstay Hotel. She and Hilary were entertaining frugally; meat being scarce, it was a pasta and farinaceous diet, enhanced with raw red Algerian wine. (We are reminded of Pym's entry in her 1940 diary when their mother had secured a seven pound jar of marmalade: "Not even love is so passionately longed for".)

Excellent Women, Pym's flagship novel, was based around St Gabriel's. Built 1853 in flaking ragstone, with Gothic finishes, it has today seen better times.

"The whole place is crumbling," shouts down a workman as he skims up the scaffolding to attend to roof repairs. Weeds and wild flowers cluster the dishevelled courtyards, the detritus of another autumn swirls against heavy doors, hinged and strapped and belted in iron. A wild web of ivy grasps a huddle of potted plants. I resolve to come to 6 o'clock evensong, as proclaimed on a service sheet, fastened to a small side door. But again I am thwarted. The church is barred. A tall man walks towards me through the dark evening, leading a Labrador. Yes, he knows the church; a peculiar church he assured me; open on Sundays, but he and his wife had long ago reverted to the Guards' Chapel.

From 1949–1961 Pym and Hilary lived at 47 Nassau Road, Barnes. A wide quiet street, flanked with fruit trees, where each villa is stamped with its own decorative feature; an apron of red gingerbread tiles, Tudor beams, latticed windows or a stained glass door surround. Barnes was the cream of suburbia and Nassau Road itself, desirably sited between Barnes Green and the Thames. A number '9' bus took them off to work. The sisters had comfortable rooms on the first floor, from where they amused themselves looking across to the neighbours' gardens. Pym derived much material in this way for her two novels: *Less Than Angels (1953)* and *No Fond Return of Love (1961)*.

Barnes was evoked in all its salubrious contours. It was particularly agreeable to stroll along the towpath, a few hundred yards from the house; the purlieu of dog owners striding purposefully ahead, with Sealyhams, Labradors and panting terriers, and cyclists deftly dodging all such impediments. On summer evenings it was the resort of young couples, entwined and swaying as the scullers skimmed the water below.

The towpath is still a bosky idyll; an overhung green tunnel of hazel and sycamore with convolvulus and waxy white laurustinus piercing the gloom. In the twilight Pym's hesitant hero, Tom Mallow: "... pulled Deirdre towards him and almost ceremoniously led her to a seat under some elderberry trees, covered with sickly-smelling creamy flowers. ' "I do love you so much," she said, "but women aren't supposed to say that to men are they?" ' They sauntered back up Nassau Road, its front gardens swathed in fuchsia and tamarisk, and heard a neighbour playing the cello and then saw a mother laying up breakfast around the baby's high chair.

"Life goes on," said Tom.

"Yes, I suppose it's comforting to see people going about their humdrum business," said Deirdre."

Fifty years later, a printed note pinned to a gnarled apple tree beside Pym's old home: 'Lost – small male ginger short-haired cat' – brings her back with a rush.

On a sunny November morning 2001, I met the present owner of the house. Mr Arvanitakis was Greek, an architect and recently widowed. He and his wife had lived there from 1975. He showed me round. Mr Arvanitakis had met Pym's landlady, Mrs Lear, fulsomely described in *No Fond*

Return of Love as 'Mrs Beltane': '. . . so scented and jingling with bracelets, carrying her little poodle, blue-rinsed to match her hair.' Mr Arvanitakis verified that the hair was silver grey, piled high and 'manufactured'; that Mrs Lear kept her Pekinese on a jewelled leash, clutched to her bosom and that she lived on the ground floor.

The two sisters had their own door and used the wide staircase up to their light, spacious first floor rooms. They kept plants on the landings and had a bedroom each, with a good sized kitchen and bathroom, a large sitting room, with an adjoining cubby hole used by Pym for writing. Her bedroom overlooked three gardens; their own, luxuriant in roses and a screen of apple trees and pear, a mature sumach tree and magnolia; all of which remain since Pym moved away forty years ago. The neighbours' gardens, now encroached on with brick extensions and conservatories have demonstrably shrunk. 'The colonial gentleman with the African mask lived to the right and at no 45, to our left, we had Paul Raymond of the Revue Bar and his mother. Mrs Raymond was attended to by a Miss Ramsbotham . . .' 'Come to the attic floor where there is an even better view.' The Edwardian red-tiled roofs of the adjacent houses blazed against the blue autumn sky and a fine cedar tree at the foot of the colonist's garden lent considerable dimension.

Hilary Pym had recently visited Mr and Mrs Arvanitakis. 'Yes, we had tea and cakes – here – in Mrs Lear's old ground floor bedroom. She found it strange seeing the house again. The tricks of memory had somehow turned the rooms back to front in her mind.'

There is a quintessential Englishness about Barnes; especially by The Green, where the agreeable little shops in Church Road bulge with mothers, toddlers and prams. Old ladies lean on shopping trolleys, their trim grey heads, like birds, stretched high on scrawny necks. Squeals from a high-walled primary school signal morning break. Tea and coffee shops jostle with baby clothes, fanciful dresses, flashy glass belts and necklaces – as revelled in by 'Penelope' the outré younger sister in Pym's *Unsuitable Attachment*, and the perennial enticement of bric-a-brac and bisque plates. The curio shop of antique adornments in *Jane and Prudence* would have been well drawn from here. 'Jessie', the modest lady companion, who spent her half-days with the roguish 'Fabian', espied a brooch. ' "All on this tray 15s," Jessie read. They went into the shop and Fabian bought the brooch, which the shopkeeper wrapped in a piece of tissue paper, evidently not thinking it worthy of a box. When they had got outside, Jessie unwrapped it and pinned it on to her mackintosh.'

A vignette that would have surely interested Pym on this late autumn morning was that of the owner of a distinguished picture gallery and his lady assistant, seated at a table in the window, eating a hot lunch. Appetising wafts of cheese and tomato spiralled up around the paintings on the walls.

And we can be assured that Mr Arvanitakis, himself, in his natural capacity as a Greek and a widower, would soon have found an effective placement in a Pym village plot.

Although the local church, St Michael and All Angels, by Barnes Bridge, would not compare with her favourite and glorious All Saints, Margaret Street. Pym was fond of it and involved herself with the Parochial Church Council. Built 1893 its light and spacious rare brick nave exudes a cherished air. On a cold autumn morning some twenty vases are positioned round the church interior, filled with fresh white roses, pink and red and a generous show of love-lies-bleeding, all clearly picked from neighbours' gardens. This Anglo–Catholic church has all the trappings that Pym enjoyed; the incense, the choir and the ubiquitous candles. 'Christmas Drinks in the Vicarage' – 'A Mardi-Gras Party' – 'Champagne Breakfast' on Easter Day – 'the Vicar's Summer Drinks Party' – 'Harvest Festival Mass' and 'All Saints Bonfire' would clearly keep all 'excellent women' busy. In a corner of the side aisle, a table and cloth is permanently set with a box of Tetley tea bags, a large round tin marked 'CAKE', a bowl of sugar, milk and an electric kettle. A comforting touch; perhaps Pym introduced it when serving on the Council. But there was one shameful incident during her stay of duty; the convivial and much respected vicar was found to have a penchant for little boys. Notes were discovered in the pockets of the choir boys and acolytes, advising on the terms for a variety of attentions rendered. Pym was deeply shocked by the sordid goings-on and was further upset by the light-hearted attitude of some of her male friends. The judge coded the case as: "The Tariff of Malpractices". A perfect title for a novel it was suggested to Pym.

A favourite walk along the river included Barnes Old Railway Bridge. In summer 1959, Pym was photographed leaning against the iron latticed parapet with her close friend, Bob Smith. After 40 years, the view from the bridge is unchanged, the 18th Century elegant terrace stands serene across the water, with the peaceful near river bank thick with willow. Pym had effectively been sent Robert Smith from Egypt in 1952, by their mutual friend, Jock Liddell. Smith had borrowed his copy of *Some Tame Gazelle* and on returning to London was determined to meet the author. At thirty-nine years, Pym felt exceptionally attracted to the younger man; his courtly manner and deep resonant voice gave him a certain dominance. He was good looking and fun and clever with lots of thick, dark hair. Perhaps wisely she did not extend this new friendship into another romance. Their lifelong relationship remained close and stimulated by many shared interests. With her fondness for younger men in mind, Smith later introduced her to the tall, dark, handsome Bahamian; the consequent implications of that exotic friendship might well have been interpreted by Pym as "fruitful".

She was touched by Smith's genuine interest in her work. He was excellent company walking and talking, lunching and letter writing and a succession of sometimes hilarious "church crawls" engendered pleasure in both their lives. A precious walk together in October 1956 had left a vivid impression on Pym. She wrote of it in her diary, and reproduced the mystique she had sensed in *A Glass of Blessings (1958)*. She and Smith had taken the towpath from Hammersmith Bridge towards Putney and had passed by Harrod's Furniture Depository. Set high above the river, it appeared forlorn, aban-doned, with bird-droppings streaking white down the rose brick walls. Pym imagined vast rooms of rotting furniture, crawling with woodworm and white ants. The adjacent pinkish ochre stone mansion loomed with a central pediment festooned with foliate garlands; 'Grinling Gibbons, decorations,' pronounced Pym.

Two years later she re-enacted the scene in her novel as Wilmet Forsyth and her perplexing admirer, Piers Longridge, walked through a misty autumn afternoon towards the Depository. 'We had not gone very far when a great and splendid looking building loomed up round a bend in the path. It was a rose brown brick, with minarets almost in Turkish style. The façade was decorated with carved swags of fruit and flowers, and there were many windows, blank and blind looking, some a little open. "What is it?" I asked in wonder. "I never expected to see such a building here." '

'It's a furniture depository,' said Piers. Wilmet's subsequent description of the river, fading pink and silver into the distance, and painterly warehouses opposite looking like palaces does not quite compare today. Although on an autumn afternoon, it is an opalescent river that laps the shale at low tide, the swans glide, the sea gulls scream and spiders swing between the tangled purple thistle and white Russian vine.

(In 1993 the Depository effectively had puppies. Harrods Village was built in the same vernacular with pink brick and yellow stone and a rash of cupolas and cobbled corners.) A young man in green uniform pops out of a pagoda. 'People used to store furniture there,' he exclaims, 'now the Depository is converted into flats – luxury flats.'

8

Africa in Fetter Lane

Pym's twenty eight years (1946–1974) at the International African Institute spanned their spacious premises in Lower Regent Street, the dust and cobwebs of St Dunstan's Chambers in Fetter Lane, to the final modern block in High Holborn. Daryll Forde, Professor of Anthropology at University College, London, infused new energy into the post-war IAI. Described variously as dynamic, brilliant, energetic and extrovert, his female staff and principally Pym and her younger colleague, Hazel Holt, were suspended in a state of fear and admiration. Hilary found him uncultured in the literary field … Holt later portrayed him as "tall, broad-shouldered and good-looking with a shock of grey hair". Pym referred to him in her letter to Henry Harvey on 5th June 1946: "I work for dear Professor Daryll Forde, who is brilliant, has great charm but no manners …"

Forde was best known for his studies on the Yakö – the villages of the Cross River in Southern Nigeria. His evocative papers on "Spirits, witches and sorcerers in the supernatural economy of the Yakö" and "Death and succession: an analysis of Yakö's mortuary ceremonial" made up a rarefied dossier towards his publication in 1964 of "Yakö Studies". Aged 32 years he had published his book *Habitat, Economy and Society*. It remains today the most descriptive and standard study of anthropology. A superb teacher, his students also found in him a great listener. But loquacious by nature, his natural exuberance often led to outbursts. According to a former student: "… he was capable of strong, if transient antagonisms and of caustic comment that on occasion reached libellous proportions."

The professor was soon to earn an ambiguous role in Pym's novel *Jane and Prudence*. 'Doctor Grampian' had, quite unknowingly, the delectable 'Prudence Bates' in his thrall. (The nature of the work in this fictive office is not made clear.) Prudence waits, in endless anticipation for his door to open – to send for her – to call her name. It is a rare occurrence. She returns from such forays "quite exhausted". Her colleague commiserates: "Contact with a brilliant mind like that must be very tiring." Prudence's patience is briefly rewarded on 'an early spring evening with the sky a rather clear blue just before the darkness came ...". Her unrequited love for Dr Grampian flared up as they sat together over a manuscript. He lay his hand on hers and said: "Ah, Prudence ..." was he going to kiss her? Sadly nothing happened. He merely retrieved his hand and said flatly: "Well, thank you, Miss Bates, I'm afraid I've kept you rather late. You'd better run along home now."

In her essay 'Novelist in the Field', Holt paints a compelling scenario of the offices she shared with Pym at the Institute. Fetter Lane, swathed in dinge and dust and cold brown lino evoked the most spartan locale. Two wooden desks faced each other in the cramped room, as Pym and Holt typed with two fingers. They would struggle in turn with recalcitrant wire trays shedding their load, with ever mounting galley proofs, and with maps spilling out of waist-high cupboard doors. Pym scooped up any sheets of old manuscripts, to use up on notes for her novels. One slack afternoon she had trimmed Holt's hair, a strand of which was later inserted into their home-made 'ju-ju'; a West African charm, to be approached in time of trouble. This Heath Robinson method in their madness induced a certain scepticism in Professor Forde. "Barbara has no sense of urgency," he would groan. But his Assistant Editor proved the ultimate professional who produced on cue the four editions of *Africa* each year.

Yvonne Cocking, former secretary to the present Barbara Pym Society, worked in the IAI in 1963 as a library assistant. In the Society journal, *Green Leaves*, she gave a vivid account of the spills and thrills at the Institute 40 years ago. She remembered such hazards as overflowing ashtrays, and cabinets bursting with storage boxes of unbound journals, along with catalogues and current research papers. The excessive weight became a danger to the flooring and had to be judiciously distributed round the rooms. Cocking revived an image of Pym sitting languidly in her office "one arm draped over the back of another chair with a cigarette in hand". Becalmed and smiling amid the piled chaos of her desk, she was always formidably in control. She ran things well. To the younger women, Pym was authoritative.

She spoke slowly, enunciating her words clearly. Cocking had never met a novelist before and held Pym in awe, who in turn was kind and sympathetic to the junior workers. Finding staff for the IAI was a perennial challenge. A Ghanaian young man was once employed in 1969. Pym wrote to Philip Larkin: "A Ghanaian we had was NOT a success and spent a large part of his day conducting endless telephone calls in his native language (Fanti, I think)." But it was in her obituary (1980), in *Africa*, that we read of Pym's candescent presence at the Institute and that engaging lopsided smile she gave to unexpected callers at Fetter Lane.

American students, anthropologists, seasoned Africanists all descended on Pym's brown lair, eager to discuss their books and articles and any future exploits in the field. Looking askance at her pile of galley proofs and books crenellating her desk, they would be promptly re-assured that their visit was in no way an interruption.

It was Pym's close friend, Robert Smith, former Professor of History at Ibadan, Nigeria and author of historical books on West Africa tribes, who regularly breached "that cobwebby building in Fetter Lane". He would take Pym out to tea – sometimes lunch – all depending on the state of the proofs and reviews. The Quality Inn in Baker Street, reached easily on the Circle Line was a convenient, if not a favourite venue. Smith recalls that the dishes on offer were optimistically "topped" with a variety of sauces. Pym adopted a special affinity with self-serve cafés. Her favourite was the Kardomah in Fleet Street, which inspired perhaps that similar affection as Peter Quennell and Harold Acton had held for the Moroccan Tea Rooms in Oxford. Pym regarded such anonymous venues as prime catchment areas for observing. She would sit upstairs in the Kardomah window and look down on the surging street scene below. (What motivated that sulky youth who stood there selling a paper – some 'Anarchist Publication' – as the scurrying crowds passed him by?) But the romantic supposition that we can never know who might walk out of the lift was lost in the basement of the Kardomah. It was not to Pym's taste. She did not find the shady table by the Gents cloakroom, where harassed looking middle-aged men and their women met secretly, conducive to her own plots. It was snatched lunch hours with Holt, surprise tea dates and Danish pastries with Smith, and all those poached eggs, and fish cakes and stewed apples that sustained those happy office hours. Years later, in August 1977, when the Kardomah was no more, Pym wrote nostalgically to Larkin: "... I always liked it [in the old August] days in London – summer dresses in the office and the visiting American anthropologists and slipping out for tea at the old Kardomah in Fleet Street." In 1970 it had been demolished and she pasted a newspaper cutting in her spiral notebook: "The Kardomah Café, Fleet Street, a familiar haunt for the legal and journalistic professions, for many years is closing..." Reported Pym: '3 July 1970 – Nellie's last day in the Kardomah. She got £5 a week part-time and had cleared tables for 22 years. In the heat of June her remark to a man customer "Oh, look at you perspiring."

In her biography – *A Lot to Ask*, Holt has portrayed its bizarre splendour: 'mosaic-covered walls – featuring peacocks with spreading tails on a sea-blue background, stained glass borders to the windows ...' In 1955 Pym had the foresight to preserve its striking art deco interior, in the introduction to her novel *Less Than Angels*. Her heroine 'Catherine Oliphant', brooding on her cup of tea, felt momentarily transported to Ravenna with those mosaics around her; – "There were large bright peacocks with spreading tails, each one occupying a little alcove, almost like a side chapel in a cathedral." Catherine noted wryly that each tray carrier was more intent on his poached eggs and a free rickety chair, than any amount of burgeoning peacocks.

In 1959, Smith left London for Nigeria, becoming something of an Africanist, with his continued lecturing and research. After his weekly meetings in London with Pym for the past seven years, he relished her monthly letters. Such random missives must have invested London with a tantalising allure.

To Bob Smith in Ibadan

40 Brooksville Avenue
9 March 1962

Dearest Bob

Excuse this Institute paper, but Friday afternoon seems a good time to write to you, as I make it a rule never to do anything that may upset me for the weekend and so like to put Africa and our irritating authors out of my mind ... Lent must seem odd in the tropics, but no doubt you are well used to it by now ... Much love. Barbara

40 Brooksville Avenue

15 December 1962

Dearest Bob,

I thought, surging through Smith's in Fleet Street today, 'I'm just a tired looking middle aged woman to all those (mostly young) people, yet I have had quite a life and written (or rather published), six novels which have been praised in the highest circles ... Love, Barbara.

IAI

11 January 1963

Dearest Bob,

I am writing this in the office on a Friday afternoon, surrounded by the raw material for the April *Africa*, the proofs of various books, and a shopping bag containing tins of cat food, frozen fish cakes, packet soups etc. ... Love, Barbara

Through the years, Pym would give Smith books from the Institute to review. She enjoyed his style and particularly his books on the Yoruba tribes. She found them more romantic than his more exacting work, *The Lagos Consulate*. With her innate sense of detachment, Pym never cared to fraternise with Africans. The temporarily engaged Ghanaian in the office had clearly proved an irritation to her. Years later when languishing on her sick bed, Smith called to see her at Barn Cottage. He had with him a visiting Fellow from the Roman Catholic Order of St Anthony. Leaving him downstairs, Smith was nevertheless warned by the discomforted Pym: "Next time don't bring any Africans." Remembering Pym in the talk at The Pen Club in 1985, Bob Smith impressed on his audience how every 'phrase and facet' in her life had been a fulfilment. She had been no frustrated spinster. Rachel Billington in her retrospective "Spinster Eye" for *The Financial Times* – July 21 1984, even hinted at lurking passions and a 'secret sexuality'. To the last of her days Pym was optimistic that a new drug would be found. Her specific prescription, she assured her visitors, sounded like 'Tio Pepe' and her doctor had told her that champagne would do her more good than Lucozade. But such bravura could be tempered by grim asides. "There is nothing I don't know about being sick ...," she finally admitted to her dear, attentive friend Bob Smith.

Today, the publication of the quarterly *Africa* is under the competent chairmanship of Dr Elizabeth Dunstan. The tradition of the Institute's cramped working space still persists. Dr Dunstan's office, to compare with a ship's galley, is perched on the fifth floor of SOAS at London University. She has direct access to all amenities and produced a photocopy of Pym's obituary in minutes.

Dr Dunstan studied linguistics and taught at Ibadan University. She remembered Professor Forde; an intense, academic man with horn-rimmed glasses. He would come out to Ibadan on IAI seminars. One night at dinner, he had ordered steak and eaten three-quarters of it with relish. Only then did he complain that it was inedible (could it have been hyena, wart hog or buffalo?). The professor was offered a second steak which he also devoured.

Dr Dunstan's constricted office evoked Holt's earlier description of conditions at Fetter Lane: "Neither of the rooms we shared at the Institute for over twenty years can have been more than eighteen feet square. Taking up most of the space were two large wooden desks, set facing each other." Today, bound volumes of *Africa* from 1928–1999 rest along one wall, balancing bottled water, packets of 'classic' dark roasted coffee and ginger orange tea. Files, bulging with maps and catalogues and manuals on anthropology and archaeology are lodged at ground level. Dr Dunstan indicated to me the 'kikalong' rubber step to reach the prized volumes towering above. Edifying articles are revealed on "African Worlds" by Daryll Forde; "Land Ecology and Resistance in Kenya 1880–1952" and "Between God, the Dead and the World" by Professor Richard Fardon (present editor of *Africa*). The more recent edition – vol. 72:1 – 2002 – has intriguing pronouncements on 'Witchcraft in the Onitsha Mission 1890'; 'Commercialising Cattle Theft' and 'Re-interpreting Kenya's Mumbo Cult'. The reader is first informed that 'the exact origin of "Mumbo" remains murky'. The serpent 'Mumbo' appears to have swallowed up and spontaneously regurgitated a number of spiritual leaders along the shores of Lake Victoria. This remarkable performance is claimed to have taken place as recently as the early twentieth Century. The resulting 'Mumboists' – (and might we attribute their 'murky' origins to their muddy conception in Lake Victoria?) – emerged as anti-colonial and sworn to change Western 'whites' into monkeys. All Europeans were discouraged from entering districts where there was 'Mumbo trouble'. Mumboists were conclusively tried and silenced in 1933.

"I just let it flow over me," Pym jotted in her notebook as she ploughed through the jargon of anthropology; its cults and rituals and emerging trends. She especially delighted in leafing through the new books for reviews and indeed the authors themselves were always of interest. She would ponder on whether 'with a little polishing' they might be insinuated into her novels. Such arresting titles as *La Polygamie au Congo Belge – Beer, Sorghum and Women* or *Strategies of Slaves and Women* must have tickled her sensibilities. Having spent a sizeable chunk of her life in close proximity to Daryll Forde, it was a shock to Pym when he died suddenly, at the beginning of May 1973.

"... at work one day and dead that same evening. It was all very distressing and we have been rather like a rudderless ship ...," she wrote to Larkin. Forde had mellowed through the years, his impertinence and short temper abated. His two cohorts, Pym and Holt rated him an exciting and stimulating leader. But it has to be recorded that on the one occasion that Forde borrowed from Pym one of her novels, it was returned with no comment.

9

Church Crawls

In May 1955 Pym went with Bob Smith to High Mass at All Saints, Notting Hill. The church is marooned in a paved esplanade; an imposing rock of rectitude, further protected by bollards and cul de sacs. Having staved off the LCC from running a highway across its bows in the 1950's, All Saints guards its space. Victorian, built in pleasing gold sandstone, All Saints lists a bleak war record, written in gold paint on a blue wood plaque in the porch:

'Church seriously damaged by enemy action and made unusable' –
26 September 1940
'Vicarage burnt out' – 27 May 1944

The Parish Hall had also sustained crippling injuries, but according to the citation, damage was repaired and church life resolutely continued. A second plaque in the porch details the parish priests. John Herbert Cloete Twisaday was by far the longest serving from 1932–1961. Smith noted that his penchant for the Low Countries had resulted in a liberal show of embroideries and pious knick-knacks. On the morning of her visit, Pym found him 'an elderly dried up celibate, irritable and tetchy'. He fidgeted in the pulpit, with disconcerting pauses in his delivery. She feared he had forgotten himself and would collapse in a fit. But she relished the High Catholic overtures and especially Asperges – the sprinkling of holy water at the start of the service.

Today, 50 years ahead on a leaden November afternoon, All Saints could not be described as an attractive church inside. The wide aisles are lit through the plain side windows and a wood pulpit surveys a stern regiment of chairs. Props for family activities are collected on trestle side tables, to reflect a busy church. A Christmas Fayre is promised:

Books
Bottles
Cake
White Elephant
Face Painting
Refreshments
and
Father Christmas

By the end of her life Pym had become disenchanted with the exigencies of Church Bazaars. But in her novels, notably *Excellent Women (1952)* they were framed with gusto. The jewels in the crown of a Church's curriculum. And in *Excellent Women* she wrote of such diversions as the Fancy Work stalls – the Hoop-La and the Bran-Tub. A photograph of her in later years shows her manning a church fête bookstall; a natural habitat.

On a June evening in 1962, hot and tired from 'late-night' shopping in Oxford Street, Pym made her way to All Saints, Margaret Street. She knew the church's cool courtyard; a haven from the din and crowds of Oxford Circus. A modest 100 ft square area with garden seats and bulbous terracotta pots of trailing greenery and flowers. Fitting the church and vicarage and choir school into this small space was the ingenious work of the Victorian architect, William Butterfield. The chequered pink and black façades are surmounted with a slate spire that can be seen from Primrose Hill. Together with her friend, Robert Smith, Pym explored many London churches. How she must have revelled in All Saints, with its bursts of gold and brilliance. The awesome High Altar with its gilded tracery and exotically draped saints, is approached by a wide nave, supported by massive pillars of red Aberdeen granite. Pym loved colour and richness; jewels and silks and velvet adorn her more auspicious heroines. The marble pulpit and font also captivate; both elaborately set with mosaics of Sienna ochre and rose, Irish green and Derbyshire fossil grey. A distilled odour of incense, lingering from one service to the next, denotes regular parish attendance. For Pym, there was 'incense' and 'incense' – as revealed in *Excellent Women*. Her manqué hero, Rockingham Napier, enquires of his quasi landlady, Mildred Lathbury: "High Mass – with music and incense? ... I hope it is the *best* quality incense? I believe it varies."

The Church of Annunciation, Marble Arch, on a weekday afternoon – is closed. I enquired from the porter of the flats adjoining, in Old Quebec Street, why it was not open as it purported to be. He was dismissive. He did not know the church's timetable. But he was next door? – "Yes, but we don't get on." High Mass was proclaimed for Tuesdays 12.30 – I went along.

A lofty grey stone interior with a wide nave. A sombre, spacious church. A Gothic style high rood screen – carved elaborately, like crisp, dark chocolate. Ornate low hanging metal lamps and a liberal supply of tall brass standard candle holders. Coloured tableaux of the stations of the Cross are hung on either side of the aisle.

A handful of communicants before the St George's Altar. No music, no incense, it was Low Mass. Brilliantly coloured stained glass windows: huge and ornate, set high above the Lady Altar and the St George's Altar. A disconsolate priest led me to the Bapistry. "Here is the most beautiful window of all; said to be by Burne-Jones. Come again when the sun is out and you will see the colours." He flapped off purposefully down the side aisle. The young Curate smiled as I turned to leave – "Barbara Pym admired this church," I said. "Oh! Yes! But of course – and there has been a plaque put up on her old house in Queen's Park."

Pym wrote in her diary April 30th 1955 how she and Bob Smith had lunched and then walked in Hyde Park through the young green trees. But Bob had needed more than nature and they dropped in to the Church of Annunciation at Marble Arch. 'Lofty but impressive with the lingering smell of incense.'

In August 1971 Pym began a letter to Philip Larkin: "How splendid All Saints, Margaret Street is – close to 200 people there!" A few days before Christmas 2001, I chanced on the vicar, Fr. Alan Moses. "Come to tomorrow's 'Blessing of the Christmas Tree'," he urged. It lay in the courtyard, its branches bound and unadorned. I took the grandchildren, Luke and Jemima, to the service. The church was a feast of gemütlich richness. Burning candles soared out of holly and ivy and the tree shimmered in strings of light and baubles. Fr. Alan Moses conducted a carol service, to include a reading of John Betjeman's poem 'Christmas':

The Holly in the windy hedge
and round the Manor House the yew
will soon be stripped to deck the ledge.
The altar, font and arch and pew . . . .

From the silver bowl beside the tree, Fr. Alan Moses next scooped out some magic with a silver ladle. Twice he tossed it over the glittering fronds. Was it incense? Myrrh? At the close of the service, we sniffed the bowl, Luke, Jemima and me. 'Just water,' muttered Jemima – '*Holy* water,' corrected Luke. The congregation – some 200 people? – crowded the courtyard, where Pym's familiar 'excellent women', banked behind trestle tables, handed out mince pies and mulled wine.

On a bright December Sunday morning I saw inside St Gabriel's, Warwick Square. The scaffolding had been removed and the lights blazed; a rejuvenated scene after that desolate dark winter's evening a month before. 'A peculiar vicar', the man with the dog had warned.

Much purposeful activity and bustle in the aisles, with priests and solid priestesses and young girls with hair plaited and coiled off their angelic faces. An altar in raspberry silk panels was set up with glowing fat candles at the head of the pews; a lectern alongside. The elegant brass pulpit – much admired by Sir Nickolaus Pevsner, the ultimate authority on art and architecture – seemed strangely detached from the preparations below. Was the pulpit too rickety to use? I later asked a priestess. No – the priest preferred to be on a level with his congregation, she explained. The chancel appeared dim and distanced. The ravishing mosaics and alabaster arcading were hard to see. The outer aisles were vaulted in gleaming wood, and above the central stone pillars, the corbel supports looked down with leonine male heads and luxuriant beards. The stained glass chancel window waited for the sun. A solemn bell tolled. Pym's second floor bedroom windows, just yards away, would have born the full impact. In her acclaimed early novel *Excellent Women*: 'I could just see the church spire through the trees in the Square. Now when they were leafless, it looked beautiful, springing up among the peeling stucco fronts of the houses; prickly, Victorian-gothic, hideous inside, I suppose, but very dear to me.' Pym's heroine, Mildred Lathbury, had also noted that the neo-Gothic interior lacked age and patina, but found comfort in the polished brass wall tablets and the air of Victorian solidity. Mildred had stepped into St Gabriel's, one morning, for solace from an emotional shock. 'I was relieved to see that there was nobody else there and I sat down hopelessly and waited, I did not know for what. I did not feel that I could organise my thoughts but I hoped that if I sat there quietly, I might draw some comfort from the atmosphere.' Pym had sought the same in the late 1940's, still lacerated from her love affair with Gordon Glover. Cavalier and handsome, she had woven him into *Excellent Women*, as the irresistible charmer, Rockingham Napier.

As I looked and waited, a chattering covey of elderly women in wool hats slowly filled the pews. The organ rolled through its repertoire. Priests in raspberry chasubles and a clashing red-headed priestess took their positions. The service of Sung Mass was pleasantly wafted along by some male tenor behind me. I imagined him tall, clearly eloquent and handsome. And then he walked up the aisle, to read the second lesson and to face his expectant audience. Dark certainly, with bristling facial hair and a fashionable black bomber leather jacket. The vicar, a Gaelic man with a pallid appearance gave a plausible résumé of Saint Augustine. He is commemorated on August 20th, concluded the vicar helpfully; a piece of information that seemed incongruous on such a freezing morning. The Eucharist evolved with a respectable show of silver chalices and little bells. I was disappointed to find the wine was white and that there was no incense. 'Very expensive,' a priest assured me after the service. 'We keep a pot specially for Christmas Day. And you should come at Easter, Harvest Festival Thanksgiving and Remembrance Sunday.'

The vicar knew all about the special connection between St Gabriel's and Pym and her novel *Excellent Women*. 'She used St Gabriel's in *all* her novels,' he told me with an air of authority. An 'Excellent Woman' in a duck-egg blue mackintosh and matching hat, handed me a cup of milky coffee.

Pym began her fifth novel *A Glass of Blessings* with a surprise; neither a nasty nor an amazing surprise, only an unequivocally strange surprise and strangely out of place. She had stepped in to a lunchtime service at St Mary Aldermary in Queen Victoria Street. Tucked into the corner of this busy road by Mansion House underground station, and reasonably close to the office, the church was another favourite venue. The vicar, affectionately known as Canon Freddie Hood, had an Oxford provenance. For many years he had been the popular principal of an Anglo–Catholic centre for the undergraduates. Bob Smith would imitate his lisp and his cheery invitations to 'shewwy wine and compline'. But what had so surprised Pym on that particular early afternoon? Let her speak:

> Chapter One – I suppose it must have been the shock of hearing the telephone ring, apparently in the church, that made me turn my head and see Piers Longridge in one of the aisles behind me. It sounded shrill and particularly urgent against the music of the organ, and it was probably because I have never before heard a telephone ringing in church that my thoughts were immediately distracted, so that I found myself wondering where it could be and whether anyone would answer it. I imagined the little bent woman in the peacock blue hat who acted as verger going into the vestry and picking up the receiver gingerly, if only to put an end to the loud unsuitable ringing. She might say that Father Thames was engaged at the moment or not available; but surely the caller ought to have known that, for it was St Luke's day; the Patronal festival of the church, and this lunchtime Mass was one of the services held for people who worked in the offices nearby; or perhaps for the idle ones like myself who had been too lazy to get up for an earlier service.
>
> The ringing soon stopped, but I was still wondering who the caller could have been, and finally decided on one of Father Thames's wealthy elderly female friends inviting him to luncheon or dinner.

St Mary Aldermary, the most ancient and distinguished of the City churches was first commented on circa 1080. Through the centuries it became the most sought after repository of the City notables and was selected by John Milton in 1663 for his third marriage. It was badly knocked about in the Great Fire of 1666. Wren took over and by 1682 had completed the re-build in the Gothic vernacular. Pevsner marvels at the fun Wren must have had with his Gothic refit of the aisles and nave. The entire interior ceiling with its fan vaulting of Wrenish ribbed and scrolled plaster, is an astonishing sight. More astonishing is the added adornment of Wren's serial saucer domes, which would seem suspended from some supernatural suction.

The soaring white stone tower was also given a finishing touch. The four stout polygonal pinnacles are a City landmark. Betjeman refers to them as 'fat pinnacles' and informs that they are 'tipped with golden fibreglass finials'. In its shadow, by Bow Lane, the small quiet churchyard beckons. A garden seat or two beside fruit trees, and flowering shrubs and the odd companionable pigeon, make a charming retreat. For Pym it would recall that other cool, green corner at All Saints, Margaret Street.

On a November morning and nearly fifty years after Pym's surprise, I stepped into St Mary Aldermary. The heavy, carved oak door was ajar. A lunch hour service for the Eucharist was to take place at 1 o'clock.

A thin sun filtered through the post war windows; the church was empty, silent; "expectant", Pym might say and the ubiquitous saucer domes were the ultimate Wren caprice. Where was the vestry door? It was to the left of the altar; small and unassuming and snugly recessed in its perpendicular arch. It was shut tight with no intimation of any life whatsoever behind it ...

"At St Mary Aldermary (Canon Freddie Hood's church) one heard the shrill whirr of the telephone through the organ music," wrote Pym in her diary on 29th March 1955. Six weeks later on 15th May, Pym questioned her diary: "WHAT IS MY NEXT NOVEL TO BE? It can begin with the shrilling of the telephone in Freddie Hood's church ..."

I knocked on the little door. What surprises could it hide? I was shocked when it opened. A pale man smothered in a rumpled sweater let me in.

"You are lucky to find me here," he said, and looked annoyed.

"Who are you?" I asked thankfully.

"I am the Treasurer, Mr Lane, Mr Stanley Lane, the Hon. Treasurer, I should say."

It was cosy in the panelled vestry.

"These walls are 1876 and the set of chairs is Charles II."

I admired his large, handsome carved fireplace.

"St Mary Aldermary took in a lot of furniture from churches demolished in the Great Fire: St Thomas the Apostle; St Antholin Budge Row and St John the Baptist, Walbrook ..."

"Might we have a quick look in your silver safe?" Along with the fireplace and his Carolean chairs, it took up a large part of the room. The Hon. Treasurer looked uneasy; nervous even. Who was this woman who had arrived totally unannounced and was now making it her unwarranted business to pry inside the safe?

"Not much in there at the moment," he said cautiously.

"But what *sort* of things?" I pressed him. "Incense sprinklers? Candle Snuffers? Flagons?"

The Hon. Treasurer heaved open the heavy Victorian safe doors to reveal a few scattered contents. Bundles of plate from the various said churches lay suitably wrapped in greyish dusters.

"Yes, now let me just show you our organ," said Mr Lane, steering me firmly through the vestry door and locking it behind him. "You see that carved door case by the west end? Late seventeenth Century. Brought over to us from St Antholin in 1874." Described by Pevsner as "a sumptuous piece", it was an eye trainer for any other treasures sent round to St Mary Aldermary from the destroyed City churches. Mr Lane dismissed the Victorian bench pews with a despairing wave; the Wren boxes had been replaced in 1876. I gazed up at the pulpit. A magnificent survivor from the 1680's, with carved cherubs' heads embedded deep in the centuries-seasoned mahogany. A scarlet Nu Swift fire extinguisher stood at its foot.

Mr Lane looked pale and shuffled from one foot to the other. He was in need of lunch perhaps, and was understandably keen to get rid of me.

"Barbara Pym worshipped here," I volunteered, "regularly."

Yes; he had heard; he had even read two of her books.

"Once at the start of a service, she heard a telephone ring."

Yes, Mr Lane remembered hearing of that too.

"She heard it ringing from the vestry."

Mr Lane stood before me with other things on his mind.

"Do you have a telephone in the vestry today, Mr Lane?"

"Yes – but it is not the same one that Barbara Pym heard," he assured me hurriedly. "We now have a more modern one."

"Could it be heard from the altar rail?"

"Certainly, it rings quite loudly. When the vestry door is open, it can be heard all the way to the west end of the church."

City churchyards in the summer lunch hours were an irresistible lure for

Pym. She found their grey green shade conducive to 'collecting her thoughts in tranquillity'. Failing to find a lettuce in Leather Lane market one day, she slipped into St Alban's, Holborn. "It seemed a cool and quiet place. Inside candles burn to St Alban ... I lit one and put money in the box." She sat on a seat in the small courtyard, surrounded by the Stations of the Cross, dutifully reading the parish magazine ... "Don't quite like to smoke or read Proust."

St Paul's Churchyard provided another rich landmark. A boys' band was playing the 'Pilgrims' Chorus' from *Tannhaüser*, and 'Land of Hope and Glory'. People sat on seats, with their lunch and knitting bunched up in their laps. Pym pottered round the back and saw pieces of broken marble piled about; friezes, urns and socles lay toppled, white and magnificent, and "good enough to eat", she recorded. She next noted a middle-aged woman, oblivious to the traffic streaming by, perched on her marble heap, sipping tea from a plastic cup – "as if on the rocks at the sea-side ..." Surveying this scene in September 1961, Pym further noted: "surely something for me here".

She and Hilary had moved to their house in Queen's Park the previous year and it was then that Pym had embarked on her ill-fated seventh novel: *An Unsuitable Attachment*. Her vignette of St Paul's was revived for the last page, when 'Rupert' stumbled over his demigoddess, 'Penelope': "Coming into the gardens he found himself among the office workers sitting on the iron chairs, some with sandwiches, others with knitting or books, and still others with their eyes closed and faces raised in the mild sunshine. Here, at the end of a row, sat Penelope, a half-eaten sandwich in her hand."

10

Philip Larkin Land

The Lincoln Wolds are cut with dykes; sodden green crops, plough and sheep are bounded by hedge and woodland. A quiet landscape, muted and misted by shoals of cloud. Philip Larkin's home country. The train slews up the wrinkled grey sleeve of the Humber and halts at Hull; the end of the line; Larkin's city. A sense of freedom always enveloped him when he arrived. The sea, the plains and wide empty air made it a good place to write. The Jazz Correspondent for *The Daily Telegraph* 1961–71, chief librarian of the University of Hull, and celebrated poet, had also maintained a 12 year blind correspondence with the novelist Barbara Pym. (She finally proposed they meet for lunch at the Randolph Hotel, Oxford.)

Larkin and Pym, 'A Romantic Sympathy'? In December 2001, Professor John Bayley gave a talk at Hull; essentially on their empathy and their shared humour. He explained how T S Eliot and L P Hartley had first perpetrated romantic empathy tending to the humorous. John Betjeman had next forged ahead to a modern romanticism in the glamour and comedy of his tennis belle Joan Hunter Dunn –

'Furnish'd and burnish'd by Aldershot sun, . . .' and his sportif Pam –
'Pam, I adore you, Pam, you great big mountainous sports girl,
Whizzing them over the net . . .'

Professor Bayley confessed that the intoxication he had felt reading Betjeman in his own Oxford days had since left him. It was to the power of Larkin and Pym, their sympathy and their humour, that he had returned. 'Humour is at the core of their genius.'

Being something of a poet himself, in his undergraduate years – writing under Oliver Bayley – the Professor was once confronted by Larkin:

"What do you think about Cargoes? I hate the last stanza and all that stuff – 'Dirty British Coaster'! Don't like it!"

Bayley attempted to mollify him with the exotic first line 'Quinquireme of Nineveh …' Larkin was a shy and tentative man, recalled Bayley, with an abrupt approach. And he could be painfully emotional. Once driving in his 'Larkinian conveyance – a tobacco Rover Sedan', listening to his wireless, he was overcome by a reading of Wordsworth's 'Intimations of Immortality' and drew up in a lay-by in tears.

Pym would conjure up ludicrous situations of comedy and romance between ordinary people; the more absurd the scenario and cast, the more she identified with her readers. Professor Bayley fell into paroxysms of laughter as he read out to his audience – a bevy of silver headed, rapt ladies in cherry cashmere – a passage from Pym's last novel *A Few Green Leaves*. It was the occasion of Emma's supper party in her cottage. A conscientious cook, she had made 'a tuna fish mousse and a French onion tart'. The lately eligible vicar Tom, was non-plussed by the mustered women; Emma herself looked dull in black and grey cotton … 'As for Daphne, Tom had long ceased to regard his sister as a woman whose clothes might be worthy of notice; sometimes he hardly even thought of her as a human being.' (Pym explained, sympathetically, that Daphne was 'saving her better clothes for her Greek holiday.') Bayley insisted that Pym never consciously meant to be funny but that her dialogue was constantly hitched to high comedy. Bayley again launched into Emma's supper party.

"Do you see many foxes here?" Isobel asked.
    "Oh yes – and you can find their traces in the woods," said Daphne eagerly.
    "Did you know that a fox's dung is grey and pointed at both ends?"
    "How fascinating,' said Adam at last.
    "That's something I did <u>not</u> know. I must look out for it when I next take a walk in the woods."

There was something sacramental about these absurd exchanges Bayley assured his audience. His eyes misted as he prised more pearls from his notes. He next cited references to the British seaside from *No Fond Return of Love* ... 'the sea came into view and was greeted with exclamations all round. It looked grey and cold, and the couple in the window remarked that they wouldn't care to bathe in <u>that</u>, thank you.' And later, '... the sun had come out in a rather watery sky and people were strolling on the promenade or sitting in the shelters reading newspapers, talking, or just sitting with that air of hopeless resignation that people on holiday so often seem to have.' Pym's slants of humour strike different chords in us. Whereas Bayley was disarmed by the above examples, my own favourite comical vignette comes in *Jane and Prudence*. A clumsy jog of a little table and Prudence's cup of tea was upset down her elegant lilac skirt in 'rather the shape of Italy'.

And Bayley emphasised Pym's respect for ordinariness, her attentions to the humdrum lives and routines make fascinating reading; that supreme self-identification with the reader sets in. The boredom of the kitchen sink and the laying of breakfast are venerated when shared with the admirable women on her page. Daily business was a comfort; a lynch pin of agreeable and undemanding life. Pym and her heroines lunched in Lyons and the Kardomah; Catherine, from *Less than Angels* derived pleasure from wine lists, which she would read out loud ... 'very old in wood and of great delicacy ... it sounds like something out of the Psalms, doesn't it,' she said.

Larkin and Pym, respectively, eschewed politics and any solemn proselytising in their works. They shared the comfort principle, so often linked to that self-parody of foibles. The clutched placebo after morning surgery, the milky drink at bedtime, the whiskey, the sherry and the successive cups of tea.

Class was addressed by Pym in deft, oblique references. Peoples' shoes were an indelible pointer to the wearer's standing. John Challow of *An Unsuitable Attachment* was demoted for his questionable shoes. His future wife Ianthe studied him closely on first acquaintance: 'only his shoes seemed to be a little too pointed – not quite what men one knew would wear.' Whereas the deceased wife, Constance, in *Jane and Prudence* was eulogised with '... all her shoes, long and narrow and of such good leather. Just the thing for the gentlewomen.' Whereas her widower, the ludicrous Fabian, was judged the ultimate parvenue for taking his umbrella on a country walk. This gentle seesaw of the lower and the upper accentuated the quintessential middle class stance of Pym's novels. The two last to be published in her lifetime: *Quartet in Autumn* and *The Sweet Dove Died*, created a dichotomy. The first denoted the lower class, verging on deprivation; the second a consistently upper class theme of worldly-wise sophisticates.

Pym's romantic inclination was love in the head and in the heart, concluded the Professor. She enjoyed falling in love at any age – and indeed *with* any age. For her, loving was fundamentally a sympathetic soul-state. It was sudden and unexpected. Ianthe, far away from her questionable John – 'admitted to herself that she loved him, had let her love sweep over her like a kind of illness ...'

11

Novels from Anthropology

Pym's affiliations with anthropology stemmed from her work at The International African Institute.

Working with Professor Daryll Forde, she had become in 1958 an assistant editor of the quarterly *Africa*. She was responsible for collating articles, selecting books for review, news columns and the attendant paraphernalia of maps and advertisements. Her friend and colleague, Hazel Holt, later recalled: "Barbara had little interest in anthropology as such and certainly none in Africa – she never expressed a wish to go there." Holt concluded perceptively that it was the ideological world of Africa and the Africanists that interested Pym. Editing other peoples' field work and research gave her the concept of their detachment; her own literary style evolved with this cultivation of detachment towards people and life.

Pym was a born observer; the quiet older sister who became the accomplished novelist; who, in the words of her Cotswold neighbour, Gilbert Phelps: "She could not help herself regarding everything around her with her cool, amused novelist's gaze ... it could be extremely disconcerting suddenly to become aware of those grey observant eyes." However peripheral and oblique Pym's links with Africa, she collected a mass of material from her involvements at the Institute. The cultures of Africa, the studies of tribes, the linguistic surveys that landed on her desk for editing, all totally absorbed her. References to the obscure Mugwe East African tribe, gleaned from the library, and such gems as 'Government in Zazzau' were slipped into her novels. She successfully aligned the skills of anthropology with her own deductions.

Charles Burkhart, a close friend of Pym's sister, Hilary, concluded in his paper 'Barbara Pym and the Africans' that she had 'transcended'

71

anthropology in her novels. 'She has made Africa come home to suburbia and found that they are the same, and in such a discovery some of her genius lies.' Pym's evoked supper parties in suburbia are roused with such tales as aborigines throwing kangaroos on the fire to cook; of visiting missionaries pouring out African customs from the village pulpit; and of a new neighbour 'back from the field' who spreads his rugs in the back garden, to beat them in the quiet of the evening. The shock and admiration induced by this Yang and Yin of African exuberance pulses through Pym's earlier books. Some of her more lonely heroines overtly welcome the colour and life of the native touch. Dulcie Mainwaring in *No Fond Return of Love* coyly considers letting her rooms to students: "... perhaps Africans who would fill the house with gay laughter and cook yams on their gas rings." Pym was no racist. Ironic and amused she sets up the choices and arguments in her provocative scenarios.

Pym's portrayals of curiosity come to a head in her last novel *A Few Green Leaves*, where each village member's persona is likened to a quasi anthropologist. The third person observer, Emma Howick, collates her cast to include her ex-boyfriend, her mother, her vicar, her doctor. The former admirer, Graham, changes under scrutiny as petulant and spoilt with a tendency to shoot a line. Emma smiles sagely as she sees him sitting by his cottage, at a little table weighed down with his typewriter and heaps of books stacked at his feet. The academic manqué.

Emma's mother, Beatrix, has made the study of the Victorian novel her quarry. Emma's approaching state as an 'old-fashioned spinster' has become a gnawing appendage to her mother's studies. Emma, aware that her unmarried state vexes her mother, taunts and notates. Yes, Graham spent the night in her cottage ... but they slept in separate rooms. He had not even brought his pyjamas and toothbrush. She laughs inwardly at her mother's rejoinder:– 'And of course a night in a cottage can't really be compared with those aristocratic Edwardian house parties with their sophisticated arrangements of bedrooms.' Emma deduces that her mother is anxious to openly encourage the relationship in order that a smidgen of romance might even yet be re-kindled.

The vicar, Tom, is depicted as a hapless widower, subsisting in a large drafty house with a drab and disorganised sister. When she deserts him for a long holiday, he hunts for hot meals from his village parishioners. Emma becomes slowly aware of Tom's oblique need of her; the comforts and conveniences of a home. Emma ticks off his prosaic attributes: " 'good-looking', 'nice', 'agreeable' and 'sympathetic.' " The downside traits detected by Emma's mother, as 'boring and ineffectual', do not detract from her resolve that her daughter must fulfil her role as a married woman.

The village doctor comes under a more comic scrutiny. Young Martin Shrubsole is seen hurrying through to his surgery, 'head bent as if he expected to receive a blow'. He suggests the 'hunted' rather than 'hunter'. His instincts re-assert themselves in the evening as he sits beside his mother-in-law. She is plump and for her preservation he has steered her away from sugar, butter, puddings and white bread. In a volte-face he considers resuscitating her carbohydrate cravings. She could drop down dead and the Shrubsoles and their burgeoning family would then have money for a larger house. In the last months of her life Pym had resorted to her primal absorption with detection and deduction. Cheerfully sitting up in bed, she had worked on this, her last novel, *A Few Green Leaves*. It was published posthumously. Her neighbour Gilbert Phelps, always the first to applaud 'Barbara Pym territory', with her nuances of village life, could identify no local resemblants in the book. She had perfected the art of concealing her tracks as well as pursuing them. Amalgamation could perhaps compare with compromise in the genius of Pym.

An osmotic slant would sometimes creep into Pym's detective sensibilities. In 1954 she conceived a passion for Denton Welch, who had been dead six years by the time she read his *Maiden Voyage*. This acclaimed debut, an account of his sixteenth year, when he ran away from Repton and joined his widowed father in Shanghai, captivated Pym. She became 'besotted' by this fledgling writer, this so fastidious and vulnerable idol, doomed to die at the age of thirty three. She devoured his journals, his poems and his two final autobiographies. Perhaps she particularly bonded with his infatuation for his doctor and his hopeless loitering outside his house. How she herself had hung out below Harvey's Oxford bedroom window... how she had lingered by Julian Amery's home in Mayfair – 'newly painted in cream and royal blue'.

Spurred on by her absorption in Welch, she tracked down his home in Greenwich. On a wet September day in 1956, she set off by bus to Croom's

Hill, number thirty four. She was gratified to see that her hero had lived in an elegant 18th Century terraced house with 'a nice front door and fanlight'. It was from here that Welch had set off on his bicycle in 1935 to visit relations in nearby Reigate. A near fatal accident with a car on the Brighton Road left him severely paralysed for the remainder of his short life. Pym settled herself on a wall opposite by Greenwich Park to gaze up at his home, venting her empathy on the younger man. The following autumn she inveigled a girl friend to drive her on a 'Denton pilgrimage, to Welch's final village home in Kent. They had consecrated the day with a 'Denton Picnic' of hard eggs, Ryvita, cheese and chocolate. Pym's friend, Bob Smith, in his reminiscences at the Pen Club in 1985, also talked of a 'Dentonian' picnic of banana sandwiches and Toblerone – "Barbara rejoiced in 'Darling Denton'."

Pym was enchanted by Welch's attention to detail; banal, eccentric or exotic. He penetrated the minutiae of things, evoking a grandeur for 'littleness'. This ethic was at the core of Pym's own novels. He was proclaimed a born writer by Edith Sitwell:- 'Mr Welch uses words as only a born writer used them. He never fumbles. In two episodes of the book, he produces, with absolute restraint, a feeling of overwhelming horror, for all that youthfulness.' Fifty years on, Selina Hastings reviewing Welch's biography by James Methuen-Campbell, asks the pertinent question: '… by Welch's early death was a remarkable artist lost? The answer, on evidence of the body of work he left behind, is, probably yes.'

From *Maiden Voyage* these typically quixotic vignettes catch the eye: 'The trains inside the station were lying close together like worms.'

Ashore on the Indian Ocean:– 'I found cowrie shells. Their little painted teeth and pink gums grinned up at me from the beach.'

On the oriental wagon-lit: 'Small jelly fish of spittle quivering on the floors in the passages and compartments.'

In an old Chinese palace: 'The black wood furniture glistened like a new bar of chocolate.'

It was Welch's homosexual stirrings and his nose for danger that gave an edge to his writing. Ultimately he had all the nebulous attributes to fascinate Pym; and it was his intangibility that brought him alive and closer to her.

Pym was no academic. Highly intelligent, talented and creative, the formal logics passed her by. Her years at Oxford were absorbed with English literature, poetry and her attendant intellectual admirers. But the theory of logic and its formal connotations interested her. She had skirted around the Anglican church, anthropology and the social throes of the middles classes in her earlier novels. After years of rubbing shoulders with librarians, professors, writers and explorers, the world of academe beckoned. Aged fifty eight, in the wasteland years of her career, she toyed with the idea of an academic novel; something different. Friends had already suggested she find new avenues; stories, a biography even. Larkin wrote encouragingly: 'How exciting to hear that you're thinking of turning your austere regard on redbrick academic life...'

For Pym it was a brave attempt against the grain. She conjured with the plot of an ambitious young ethno historian plundering private papers. His graduate wife, full of apprehensions, complies with his treachery. But, any germ of academe is soon submerged in Pym's endemically comic character studies; Coco, the dandy homosexual, drooling over his mother's pearls, pretentious professors and whimsical old women. The central figure, Caroline, emerges as a drifter in an unfamiliar world; written in the first person, she can be interpreted as Pym herself, feeling her way through her own wilderness years. Pym played with the novel; unconvinced she switched the first narrator to the third person and then finally let go.

Charles Burkhart in his chapter 'Miss Pym and the world of her novels', gives credit to her literary executor, Hazel Holt, for her shaping up of the manuscript. The novel was published posthumously in 1986, under Holt's good title *An Academic Question*. Robert Liddell made no mention of *An Academic Question* in his incisive guide to Pym's novels in his book *A Mind at Ease*. There could be no more consummate put down.

12

Rejection

On March 24th 1963, a sobering fourth Sunday in Lent, Pym had nursed her shock from Cape's hammer blow. To be so irrefutably rejected by one's publisher after the attention of over a decade was a glaring humiliation. She compared her pain to a lover walking out. The black and white cat 'Tom Boilkin' stirred in her lap as she sat numbed in her North London drawing room. A coal fire in the grate, scattered tea things and the Sunday papers denoted all the trappings of a quiet weekend. The forsythia was breaking out. Would it have been easier to accept bad news in the autumn or winter, she wondered, with the smell of bonfires. The maxim that in distress there is a murmured blessing was lost on her that evening and not one of her mentors or admirers could have foreseen the long 'years of neglect' ahead. Liddell opined that *An Unsuitable Attachment* deserved its congé; he felt Pym needed a pause of two or three years; "she had temporarily written herself out". He went farther: if the fated seventh novel had been published it would have made a "miserable after piece"; and bad reviews could have prejudiced any future work. Pym wrote to Larkin at length, ending on a lame premise: ". . . of course it may be that this novel is much WORSE than my others . . ." Larkin replied in a conciliatory appreciation of the novel. He had found it amusing and interesting with the mild reservation that the trip to Rome should not set a precedent for too many foreign excursions. "I think one of your chief talents is for recording the English scene." He had not much cared for the two contenders – Ianthe and John – in their 'Unsuitable Attachment'. They were unconvincing and the book was weakened at times by a loose organisation of the whole. He suggested she send it to Faber's with his recommendations. On the other hand, perhaps she would prefer "to reserve what puny effort I can make in their direction for a later book".

Larkin finally deduced that it was Cape's fear of costs and lack of profit that had led to their refusal to publish *Unsuitable Attachment*. "I should think it is probably a matter of money, like most things." The previous year Liddell had seen danger signals at Cape and had prudently crossed over to Longmans. His friend, Francis King, had warned him that Cape staff and their authors were withdrawing. And Tom Maschler, the senior editor, who admired Liddell's travel books had said to him: "... but who wants to read travel unless the author is going round with a lioness on a leash or something?" This zeitgeist for sensationalism was zestfully courted in the 1960's. As Pym herself admitted, the more provocative publications and media-embellished events, such as the Profumo scandal, left no corner for her staid, quiet sagas.

The letter from Wren Howard, director of Cape, sent March 19th 1963 weighed heavily on Pym:

Dear Miss Pym,

I feel that I must first warn you that this is a difficult letter to write. Several of us have now read, not without pleasure and interest, the typescript of your novel *An Unsuitable Attachment*, and have discussed it at considerable length, but have unanimously reached the sad con-clusion that in present conditions we could not sell a sufficient number of copies to cover costs, let alone make any profit. All costs have now increased so much ... our difficulties in publishing fiction have also greatly increased ...

You will, I am sure, appreciate how distasteful it is for me to have to write to you in this strain after publishing your novels and always having maintained a particularly friendly author/publisher relationship, but in fairness to one's company and to my colleagues I feel I cannot do otherwise.

Writing to Bob Smith in Ibadan, she admitted to "... moments of gloom and pessimism when it seems as if nobody could ever like my kind of writing again ... I get depressed about my writing and feel that however good it was it still wouldn't be acceptable to any beastly publisher." Smith assured her that her forte was to create comedy and richness from the commonplace.

And had she forgotten that "unperceptive ass who thought that *Excellent Women* was a depressing book about washing up?"

Pym's prevailing shame and hurt was compounded by Hilary's own amazement at Cape's blunt dismissal; she would always refer to the editor's letter as "chilling". Together they struggled through that perishing winter of 1962/63; purportedly the coldest in Britain since 1740. Snow lay in great swathes across the country, from Boxing Day until March, with harbours and estuaries locked in a frozen sea. The sisters were crouched endlessly on cold knees filling their paraffin stoves. Pym wrote to Larkin. Were his pipes frozen? Were they all condemned to eternal cold and drudgery? Larkin replied blandly that he always felt London to be very unhealthy; that he could hear "fat Caribbean germs pattering after me in the Underground". Although their close correspondence of 17 years had only ever engendered the prosaic 'Yours ever' and 'best wishes', Pym had a knack of probing Larkin's pain and neuroses. Every irritation and discomfort was aired between them. He wrote in February 1964: "'You will be amused to know that I passed my driving test on 3rd February – it was an extraordinary experience, and a quite unexpected outcome, as no one who had ever sat in a car driven by me held much opinion of my competence. I suppose I had an easy run – no traps or crises – and as I liked the examiner so much better than my instructor the test was quite restful. However I am now faced with the fearful onus of <u>buying a car</u> – aren't they all ugly! And small, or else terrifyingly big! ..." Thirteen years later he was to jot on the back of a Christmas card, 'A fortnight ago ran into the back of car in front and lost my no claims bonus – oh, aren't you lucky! Haven't stopped shaking." Dirt and disorder bothered him. On a postcard from North Uist, he complained to Pym: "Am among the furthest Hebrides, which is v. pretty but well littered with old tyres and rusty oil drums which this picture unaccountably doesn't show. Ferries are all late ..."

He would muse on death and depression and the unhappiness of memories; there were 12 that still plagued him in the small hours with "shame, pain and remorse". Towards the end of her life Pym had urged him to send her his poem on death. She read it with "immense pleasure and enjoyment" but preferred herself to think of new clothes through the sleepless hours or even plan a scene in a novel. In *The Observer*, 1983, just two years before he himself died, Larkin summarised his views in his terse article "Point of No Return": "Death is the end of everything, and thinking about it gives us a pain in the bowels."

Another protagonist for tradition and good behaviour had passed through London in that freezing winter of 1963. From his warm confines on board the *Queen Mary*, Noel Coward had confided to his diary on January 12th: "I have enjoyed my two weeks in London on the whole, but it has been bitterly, bitterly cold." He went on to confess that he was "sick of general 'commoness', sick of ugly voices, sick of bad manners and teenagers and debased values".

The very instances with which Pym had just concurred for her future cut and thrust copy. But for the ensuing six months, she tried hard to re-launch her baby.

For Pym, 1963 was a roller-coaster year of the good and the bad; of slammed doors and new vistas, disillusionment and fresh chances. Principally it was the year that she steeled herself to take a harder line with her novels and more especially with her heroines. They had been summarily spurned but not condemned irretrievably. She resolved to create a tougher frame for more sinuous and sophisticated role models, delving far from the village green, to brush instead with shades of ugliness and death. "Be more wicked, if necessary," her former editor had once advised. And with Proust's dictum in mind of going over characters and making them worse, Pym conceded that "to write about people's less than admirable qualities than chronicle their virtues is more interesting". Writing to Larkin in the devastation of her rejection from Cape of *An Unsuitable Attachment*, she ended on a sanguine note: "It ought to be enough for anybody to be Assistant Editor of *Africa*, especially when the Editor is away lecturing for six months in Harvard, but I find it isn't quite."

Disciplined to a lifetime of writing up her notes and diaries, Pym kept faith with her 'excellent women'; ideas and observations had been assiduously filed for future novels. She was devoted to her former protégées; had steered them into unpredictable romances, only to be tenderly retrieved, or occasionally swept into questionable marriages. An umbilical cord had linked Pym to her favourite heroines; each character had clearly reflected facets of her own persona. Mildred Lathbury in *Excellent Women* was modest, mousy and timid, sheltering in the sidelines from her secret infatuations. Pym relished sharing with her the disgust and fascination at the state of the neighbours' cluttered kitchen: '... a saucepan of potatoes which had boiled dry and were now sticking to the bottom in a brownish mass ... there were two bottles of milk, each half-full, an empty gin bottle, a dish of butter melting in the sun and a plate full of cigarette stubs.' If Mildred was diffident in her social approaches, given a slut's kitchen, she could set to with aven-geance. Pym often used the sink as a cathartic prop in those earlier novels. In his article 'How Pleasant to know Miss Pym', written for the literary journal *Ariel* in 1971, Bob Smith stressed that '... Miss Pym was the first in the field in the preoccupation with the kitchen sink, over which her female characters so often come into their own.' Romances and recalcitrant love affairs thrashed out over mops and suds, with scant attention to the job in hand, were satisfactorily smothered or set to blaze. In Pym's third novel *Jane and Prudence* we read:

> Prudence laughed and then looked a little apprehensively at Jane who was swishing the wine glasses about in an inch or two of brownish water at the bottom of the bowl ... "Oh Prudence," she said, turning to her friend with a little dripping mop in her hand.
>   "You and Fabian must make a fine thing of your married life ..."
>   "He hasn't asked me to marry him yet", said Prudence
>   "Why don't you ask him?" said Jane recklessly.

And in Pym's novels the men were always kept well away from the sink and its hallowed intrigues.

Prudence Bates, the romancer and adventuress was half-feared by Pym but equally envied and admired. "Laurence and Henry and Philip ...' The girl had an insatiable range – to closely reflect Pym's own tally of lovers. She had noted in her 1940 diary an infatuation for Julian Amery; the younger man and the homosexual were to become an attraction in her middle years.

Wilmet Forsyth of *A Glass of Blessings*, the fifth novel, was a self-contained and more sophisticated heroine. Intermittently bored, frustrated, detached, she was nevertheless an astute observer and displayed a fashionable toler-ance for sexual flexibility. Pym closely identified with Wilmet, her fastidiousness and her sanguine acceptance of things; of the potential lover's failure to comply sexually or even sartorially; (he wore a duffel coat) and of his final shacking up with 'Keith', whose short dark hair bristled like a porcupine. Pym had seen it all, felt it all, survived it all. Like Wilmet she took pleasure in all feminine enhancements, such as an ensemble of 'a pale coffee brown with touches of black and coral jewellery'. One May morning she walked Wilmet through the Temple to meet her manqué lover. She wore a simple dress of deep coral poplin, with coral earrings mounted in silver. Wilmet's comments direct us to Pym: "I always like myself in deep clear colours, and I felt at my best now and wondered if people were looking at me as I passed them." When Wilmet stayed away with friends she was enchanted by such finishing touches as 'a tablet of rose-geranium soap in the wash basin', or tea in the pretty drawing room; preferably just she and her hostess alone, with the children spirited away by nurse. And for such civilised visits she undoubtedly wore her 'new dark grey suit with my marten stole and a little turquoise velvet hat'. So gracefully equipped, Wilmet (and Pym) were made aware of all surrounding refinements; well polished mahogany furniture, delicate porcelain, finely moulded fire places and cornices. Not being privy to such interiors herself or to notable jewellery or rich clothes, Pym had indulged in Wilmet as a conduit of her own fanciful desires. However Pym herself was an accomplished dressmaker and would browse through the stores for dress materials, with changeable English summers in mind. "Lime and black cotton (to make a dress)" and a "charcoal grey suit", an assortment of gloves and a "peacock blue poplin dress" were the rudiments of her wardrobe 'Spring-Summer 1954'.

Wilmet with her marked composure towards her admirer's male lover was a forerunner for the steely Leonora; Pym's ultimate study of a calculating woman in her later novel, *The Sweet Dove Died*. This new-fashioned cool and exacting heroine is pitched into scorching imbroglios entirely provoked by her own guile.

The more Pym's later afflictions mounted up, the more she immersed herself in her books and characters. They were her continuum of life; her spur to succeed and create. In her sixty-first year she wrote again to Larkin; she felt that she had done so little in her life: "... only six novels published no husband, no children". Larkin replied with his customary cheer: "Didn't

Jane Austen write six novels, and not have a husband or children?" Pym's novels had effectively become her children; her favourite heroines, Mildred Lathbury, Prudence Bates and Wilmet Forsyth were awarded idiosyncratic encores in successive novels. In *Jane and Prudence* a small captive audience was told by the perennial villager, Miss Doggett, that "Miss Lathbury has got married … an anthropologist … his name is Mr Bone."

Prudence made a skittish come-back in *A Glass of Blessings*. Wilmet's stolid husband, Rodney, had met her in an office canteen. Finding her both intelligent and attractive, he had taken her out to dinner. Prudence, rising to the bait of yet another adventure, had inveigled him on to her Regency sofa. "How uncomfortable," murmured Wilmet … "Regency furniture isn't exactly cosy." Wilmet herself had had a most gratifying revival in Pym's sixth novel *No Fond Return of Love*, with all her stage props in attendance. She was remarked upon by sightseers at a Devonian castle. 'A tall elegantly dressed woman of about thirty five, with a fur stole draped casually over her dark grey suit …' Wilmet had retained her retinue of men; husband Rodney, doting admirer, Piers, and his young appendage, Keith. They swept her up into a waiting car, leaving the intrigued on-lookers, half-envious and half-jeering at her absurdly high heels. (In his *Tatler* review of the novel, Siriol Hugh-Jones admired "Miss Pym's pussycat wit.)"

In the autumn of 1960, the Pym sisters had moved from Barnes to North London. Hilary had found and subsequently bought a handsome late Victorian villa in Brooksville Avenue across the road from the green expanses of Queen's Park. They were led to it by dint of a detective 'saga' they had been concocting together from observing two neighbours in Nassau Road. "Bear" and "Squirrel" and an itinerant interloper they named "Paul" had given them hours of speculation and intrigue as they watched their movements from their wide first floor window. On Sundays 'Bear' would emerge in a cassock. The sisters finally hired a car and Hilary, doggedly at the wheel, followed him from Barnes across London to Queen's Park – and to the church of St Lawrence the Martyr (since demolished). To their surprise and amusement, the sibling sleuths saw that 'Bear' was the organist.

A quiet residential street, Brooksville Avenue appears a prototype of Nassau Road. The terrace of villas with their walled front gardens are shielded in lavender, clambering jasmine, clematis and fuschia. Fruit trees line the street and no 40 stands tall, with its fine, solid façade, its deep eaves and bay windows with a finial poised on the pitched front roof. The sisters had opted for the first floor room as their drawing room, for the light and for close observation of the street below. The lawns of Queen's Park are seen from the house, to include a decorative painted Victorian bandstand. There is a perpetual lull and rustle from the old chestnut trees, ash and plane clustered in the area.

Brother Gabriel Myers, from Washington DC, when on his extensive Pym pilgrimage in the late 1990's, noticed "a tree-like plant" in the first floor window. He made a spirited report: "The figure of a woman appeared in the upper window where the Pym sisters once sat. She was tall and friendly-looking, apparently not cross she smiled and nodded briefly before disappearing ... I was not quick enough to notice whether her smile could be described as 'charmingly lopsided'." He later learned that the house belonged to two men. Some ten years after Brother Gabriel's evocative visit, I was having tea with Luke Gertler and his friend, Francis, in that fabled first floor room. A coal fire burned in the grate and that same green plant almost masked the window. It was 'a weeping fig', I was told and later they showed me a narrow linen cupboard, where Pym had kept her manuscripts.

Hilary Walton (née Pym) and Luke Gertler had been colleagues at the BBC. When she heard he was looking for a house they arranged the sale in tandem with her purchase of a retirement cottage near Oxford.

"They were very poor," confided Gertler. "These rooms were drab and cold; not a lot of furniture; no central heating. Barbara did not make much money from her novels." He showed me a small bookcase of all her first editions, fondly assembled. Had he preferred any one of her novels? "*Quartet in Autumn*. I found it very moving – with my own old age approaching." Ventured Francis, "Barbara was a shy and retiring lady; slim, always nicely dressed, nicely done hair. Hilary was the jolly one."

The house today glows with colour and Victorian tastes; to reflect perhaps the rich and harmonious paintings of Luke's father, Mark Gertler. The picture rails are used to effect and wall space is decked with a collection of delectable Victorian water colours, original drawings and book illustrations. I admired the anaglypta dado running through the house. "We had it painted 'antique burgundy'," said Francis. "When the Pym sisters lived here it was all a dreary dark brown." The sisters' bedrooms, each with its period fire place have a colourful view over the back gardens; a likely catchment area for Pym's sharp eye. Thirty years ago, Gertler had hung the dining room with crimson damask wall paper; a rich backdrop for his father's vibrant paintings. "We have kept a lot of the little old brass door handles. Barbara and Hilary were pleased to see them still here." The house now exudes an ambiance of stylish Victorian comfort – or was it 'old Vienna'. Luke Gertler, tall and spare with his ascetic good looks, has re-invented his Austrian provenance.

The kitchen, so dark and cramped in the Pyms' day is now opened up with a window onto the garden. Francis pulled a steel gate across a side window; after their third burglary in 1963, Pym wrote to Bob Smith: 'We have had another burglary and are going to have a metal folding gate across the kitchen window, which is where they get in. This time they took decanters and candlesticks." We stepped into the sunny garden, where grass has given way to paving, an ornamental pool and planted tubs. The neighbour over the garden wall remembered the Pym ladies, and more particularly their cats. "I was only a boy when 'Tom Boilkin' and 'Minerva' played with our old cats 'Tim' and 'Twinks'. When the ladies went out for the day, 'Tom Boilkin' would prowl across the wall and settle himself in our kitchen."

A cast iron plaque hangs below the upper window:

Barbara Pym
1913–1980
Novelist lived here
1960–1972

It stands a proud presentation from the present owners of 40 Brooksville Avenue and the neighbourhood. Recalled Hilary, "In our day we were considered the wrong side of Maida Vale."

It was at Brooksville Avenue that Pym forged through her annus horribilis; the rejections of her seventh novel and the burglaries had turned her world bleaker. Such unprecedented body-blows had damaged her self-confidence. She felt a failure; a lost force. The subsequent years were to prove a mixed chalice; her romance with a younger man waned and ended in anguish and a mastectomy loomed. It was to friends and letter-writing that she turned; her humour and that resourceful talent to amuse sustained her. Doggedly she filled her notebooks with terse observations of déclassé behaviour and the sexual mores of the day; the roots of her future endeavour, these notebooks held the out pourings of her love and pain.

Pym's pocket spiral notebooks come in all colours – red, lemon, pale blue, ration book green and lilac. They form the crux of her fleeting thoughts, moods and scenic vignettes and her persistent preoccupation with the human race; a crammed hotch potch from trips abroad, lists for spring clothes, summer clothes, food shopping lists and a list of friends to be sent postcards back home. Household lists jostle with any fanciful details en passant; an inscription on a tomb stone: "... who fell asleep March 29th 1946 aged 72 years. Sunshine passes, shadows fall, but love and REMEMBRANCE OUTLASTS ALL." And next she is scribbling in bed on some advantages of "Being ill – an excuse to play patience and eat bread and milk, fruit jelly, Bovril and dry toast, dry toast and butter – boiled eggs. Lent – is whale meat or fish?" She then recalls, "the ride in the taxi – me sitting on the edge of the seat." And "the overdressed women at Hurlingham, in furs, veiled hats, pearls, dark nylons and platform shoes ..." In 1950, we read a composite food list with prices:

C'flakes	5/6½	
Marm		
Nescafe	1/11½	
Sticks	1/3	
Cake	2/-	
Bread	3/¼	
W'cleaner	3	1.3
		10.9
Laundry	8/11½	1.13.9

A germinal plot for a novel competes on the opposite small page: "If the Curate is married the women can gather round the young Conservative candidate instead." A single line "Early June – drenched peonies in English gardens" might evoke her war time strolls at Exbury. In 1953, June, July, we read through vivid picture narratives of France: "Amboise – our first glass of

Vouvray almost levelled us out and we slept heavily." (Charles VIII, 450 years previously, had struck his head on a low doorway at Château d'Amboise and expired.) Recovered from their hangover, Pym continued: "Lovely drive thro' the twilight, green trees and quiet villages and some country almost like the Berkshire Downs" and on to "Fougères – charming and small, but really feudal-looking with pointed turrets". On Saturday 27th June: "We had a five course lunch – melon, salami, little pieces of fish in a kind of tomato sauce, chicken and beans and apricots." Monday 29th: "Went to Chenonceaux in the morning. A little disappointing because it seems unfinished at one end, but the arches over the water are lovely. A showery sort of day." The following summer, armed with her copy of *Maiden Voyage*, Pym did a tour of Portuguese villages: "Donkeys with panniers much used – heaps of red-gold maize – cobs spread out in the sun – Mimosa trees – marrows and pumpkins, old windmills in the hills. A nun going down to the beach with a herd of little girls in pink dresses and straw hats." Next a surprise entry of "the Englishwoman (about 50). She appears savagely sunburnt with a "rather scraggy neck" in a low-cut dress. She wears sunglasses and a scarf on her head. Her nose is peeling – NB. This is me, on the last morning of Foz do Arelho." A bleak entry in February 1956 has her: "staying at home with a cold. Walking in Barnes and Putney Commons, a darkish afternoon but with a little weak sun. A rather derelict looking house with a stone squirrel in the garden." Five years later the forlorn squirrel is recovered in Pym's novel – *No Fond Return of Love*. Our heroine is tracking down her romantic ends: "The house for sale had nothing remarkable about it except a small stone squirrel, perched on a rockery in the front garden, a rather worn-looking creature with its paws tucked up appealingly under its chin." It was the unremarkable little images that seized Pym's eye, to be remembered and later embellished in a book.

June 1966 found Pym and Hilary holidaying in Greece, skirting the Aegean coastline. The sheer density of the ubiquitous olive groves irritated Pym. She complained in her notebook: "The nightmare of the olive groves and how easily one could get lost in them." But she was cheered to hear the cuckoo in Delphi and found the drive through the Thermopylae mountain pass to Lamia – "sensational". After the interminable slow haul and the descents, the driver (whom Pym describes as "a younger, benevolent

Stalin"), makes a boisterous entry to Lamia with "triumphant paeans" on his horn. In June 1969 Pym and Hilary were again in Greece. Hilary had a passion for Greece, fostered perhaps by her ex husband who had read architecture at Cambridge and done a survey in Greece in the 1930's. Her accumulated knowledge of the country had resulted in her acclaimed book: *Songs of Greece: a companion for travellers* published by *The Sunday Times* 1968. This following summer the two sisters travelled to Athens by bus from Belgium through Germany, Austria and Yugoslavia. Pym amused herself with secretly framing the passengers. The Cockney couple, the young loving couple, "the wandering scholar" who had diarrhoea, the commanding old roué "always at the bottle" and the unfortunate Irish lady who wore "unbecoming beige slacks". She and Hilary stayed at the Pension Penelope. Pym relished its air of debilitated elegance – "in need of repair and redecoration". She noted the little idiosyncrasies; plastic bowls in the bathroom for soaking the wash; all meals in rooms. Observed Pym with a hint of satisfaction: "Every inhabitant has his or her own little corner of chaos."

Their own room had a fine view of the Acropolis, with a family of cats nestled down on the opposite roof. They met up with Robert Liddell, who for some years had been Head of the English Department at Athens University; his companion, Guido, a handsome cultured Italian, joined them on their evening sorties. Life would muster round the tavernas where vivacious and ingratiating locals would play their guitars and bouzoukis. Pym was entranced by the scents from surrounding shrubs and gardens and the oranges hanging from trees. With her percipient eye for possibility she wrote in her pocket book: "Here a middle-aged English or American lady might be picked up by a young Greek adventurer." She described an especially attractive young man; one, Petros, and a student of Liddell's: "He sang songs to his guitar ... a strikingly good looking young man, tall, brown hair, strong features ... we were all out on the roof where we'd been dining." On such a night, returning to the 'Penelope', Pym dipped into her handbag to find her passport missing. "Horror!" After a protracted and fruitless search the next morning with "long waits in stuffy little rooms for help that never came", she repaired to the British Consulate. 'I'm afraid this is going to ruin your holiday,' said the man (English) in a satisfied tone. She and Hilary finally reovered it at the American Express exchange. "Oh the relief!"

Ordeals, pleasures and the 'stimmung' of travel, all impelled in Pym a fundamental need to record and confide. Her note books were her life-line through the wilderness years of non-publication; they were her identity of ongoing self esteem. And pencilled through these little pages, her ups and downs have open sesame.

13

Pitched Against the Tide

Indignant and angry at Cape's cavalier censure, Pym posted *An Unsuitable Attachment* first to an agent; it was shortly returned. She then posted it to Longmans – again returned. Next, with the lemon groves of Ravello in mind, and her diary entry of "the little bundles of dried lemon leaves which you unwrap to reveal a few delicious lemon-flavoured raisins in the middle" – Pym substituted the title with *Wrapped in Lemon Leaves*; it was sent off to Macmillan and summarily returned. Robert Liddell, despite his tepid forecasts suggested she wrote to Gollancz and Hutchinsons, mentioning his name. Pym next revised her novel. She enjoyed the process of cutting and polishing and was aware of the weakness in *An Unsuitable Attachment*, notably the liaison between Ianthe and John. They were both too sketchily defined, too tentative and dysfunctional in their courtship and, worse, they were both too incorrigibly 'nice'. The impecunious librarian's love for the upper class spinster, sprinkled with the Pym mould of churches, cats, to include a parish exodus to Rome, had potential but lacked shape. Despite Pym's tweaking and tinkering, *An Unsuitable Attachment* was to wait 20 years for publication, posthumously, in 1982. Reviewed in *The New York Times* by the novelist and critic, Edith Milton, she assessed *An Unsuitable Attachment* as "a celebration of unsuitability". She cited the parish expedition to Rome, rushing off to find an English teashop, as soon as it had set foot in the Holy City, as a hilarious example. "*An Unsuitable Attachment* is a paragon of a novel," she concluded. "Certainly one of her best; witty, elegant, suggesting beyond its miniature exactness the vast panorama of a vanished civilisation." A further American review by the intuitive Mary Cantwell also enthused: "Barbara Pym is akin to seeing an unsuspected butterfly dart out of a closet. *An Unsuitable Attachment* is vivid, sly and hard to net, and why her publishers turned it down can be clear only to them and God."

This novel will always have its protagonists and its detractors. And no author could have fussed more over a recalcitrant child. In Pym's note books alone she had recorded over thirty alternative titles: *"A Plate of Lemons, The Lemon Leaves, A Lemon Spring, Under the Lemon Leaves, A Prospect of Lemon Leaves, Hidden in Lemon Leaves."*

And in no other novel had she penetrated so deeply into the vulnerable foibles and fears of her cast. In his retrospective essay: "The Rejection of Barbara Pym", Philip Larkin insisted that there was much to cherish in *An Unsuitable Attachment*. "It is still richly redolent of her unique talent."

Back in the 1960's, Pym bowed to her critics; to the changed world of cash strapped publishers and to the acceptance world of a free-range moral code.

A catalyst, in the form of a new, fond relationship, propelled Pym into her next novel. In the summer of 1962, Bob Smith had introduced Pym and Hilary to his young Bahamian friend, Richard Campbell Roberts. He had made an immediate impression. "We did like him so much and hope to see him again." They were next invited to dinner at his Bayswater flat, in December, along with a coterie of young male actors and a Siamese action painter. Roberts, nicknamed "Skipper" by his friends, was to open up the art and antique world to Pym. "A very rich field," she wrote to Smith and speculated on her chances of writing a "Romance of the Sale Room". The antique shops and auction rooms as revealed by her new admirer proved a vivid inspiration for her next novel: *The Sweet Dove Died*. And Roberts was set to evolve as a central stimulus to the tale. By May 1963, "Skipper" had become more attentive and Pym was acutely aware that this handsome hunk of a man, oozing charm and a glamorous life-style, had captivated her. He invited the sisters to an evening view of Thai paintings – "He brings a bit of joy into life," noted Pym. Knowing that he was 18 years younger than her and a homosexual, she felt tacitly exonerated from any sexual involvement. It was her need to love that was fulfilled and that emotional interchange of the head and the heart. "Supper with Richard. We eat cosily in almost total darkness (one candle)". There were many such trysts in the flat in Sussex Gardens. He took her to the Royal Opera House, where Pym was especially interested that he crunched up his ice in the Crush Bar. She savoured the red and the gold and the intimacy of the dimmed auditorium. Pym's sensibilities were trained on her novel: 'Leonora' and 'James' – they shadowed her pleasures. How would it be for them? "A happy evening," she wrote in her diary – "May Day 1964" and speculated to herself: "If 'they' went to Covent Garden Leonora would like to feel the touch of his sleeve against her bare arm (but that would be as far as it would go)." On June 2nd, it was again "dinner with Richard at his flat" for her 51st birthday. Champagne and a lovely present. A Victorian china cup and saucer. "The Play Fellow" – a lady and her cat.' Pym was happily enamoured all that summer. "My dearest Skipper" would drive from Sussex Gardens and whisk her up to the hills of Hampstead Heath.

They would park in elegant Church Row and stroll through the early evening past the poignant Huguenot cemetery and into the little romantic churches. Skipper would light a candle but Pym refrained. "It is a bit too much like something in a BP novel," she recorded in her note book. To Windmill Hill and to Galsworthy's house, where he died in January 1933 – noted Zacharias Von Uffenbach in his Pepysian chronicles *London in 1710*. 'The district is very pleasing and, if one looks from one hill over to the other, the prospect over the Thames and London is vastly agreeable." Pottering along the 18th Century terraces, Pym and Skipper enjoyed peering in at the uncurtained windows and they talked long over cups of coffee in the high street bars. But Pym sensed a new moodiness in Skipper; there were constraints between them and that racking of the brain for what to say next. She seemed not to amuse him although he had found her books witty and sad. He was unhappy; he was losing interest? Should she leave him alone? End it all? She ended her letter: "No more of those sad looks that cut me to the heart, Skipper dear. But love anyway, Barbara"

Hilary, returning to Brooksville Avenue, from Greece where she had been enjoying an extended holiday, gratis the BBC, was alarmed to find her sister in "a romantic haze". She warned Pym tactfully "to be her age".

Finally it was Skipper who instigated a tack in their relationship. Setting off on a trip to Greece and Turkey, he briefed Pym to view and subsequently bid for some bird prints at Christie's. On a second, more formidable mission, she bid for and secured Sharpe's two volumes of *Birds of Paradise* for £1,000. She relished the bustle in the saleroom's basement, where a man sat calmly correcting proofs in the midst of chaos. A distinguished Italian had walked in, enquiring after books he had purchased months before and now could not be found. Pym became more and more adept at her assignments. She reported to Bob Smith "Miss Pym is still frequenting the sale rooms – a week or so ago, R pushed me into the end of a sale at Sotheby's – made me bid for a book on the Bahamas for him, which I got." The scenario of her new romantic novel was shaping up. These forays into the salerooms with their legendary display of objets d'art and vertue, porcelain, tapestries, books and manuscripts fuelled Pym's imagination. Perceiving her enthusiasm, Smith took her along to Bourdon House in Davies Street to feast on their most exclusive treasures: ("A rather superior antique shop") she wrote blithely to Skipper – at 6.45 am before hurrying off to work at *Africa*. "It was a rich experience, my first visit and should be used in some fictional setting. Of course there were several things I should have liked – a nice pair of mirrors 295 guineas, I think. Even the smallest malachite egg was 7 gns."

The intensity of their romantic friendship waned through 1965. On February 18th, Thursday, she confided in her note book: "A bit annoyed with R, so let us think of other things". "No word since Saturday but I just sit tight to endure."

On Monday 5th April:

But it is so terribly difficult
and now I begin almost to
worry, though I know he
must be alright. What am
I meant to do? Just go on
and on like this? Today
is so painful, I feel raw all
over. This morning I almost
definitely decided to call a
three months truce and silence –
when he gets in touch –
now tea time. I'm not sure.

A few pages on, an unfamiliar and sloping backward hand in blue ink, proclaimed

"Richard"
Hilton Hotel, Istanbul
19–25 June

On the 13th June, perhaps even over a cup of tea, Skipper had divulged to Pym his holiday dates. Pym sensed she had been 'off-loaded'; the odd friendly telephone call and respective invitations to supper, resulted in awkwardness and growing caution. What had she expected? As her prescient friend, Robert Liddell wrote: "Nothing, of course, could come of it." But something did. It was the inspiration of her most deeply felt novel *The Sweet Dove Died*. The love that she had thrust on Skipper proved her swansong. And like her former cherished heros, he was destined for fictive posterity .... as in the art of taxidermy.

It is an amusing exercise to trace the vagaries of a novelist through the build up of the plot, the venues and the characters. With her zeal for netting the moment, Pym's note book and diary entries gave an immediacy to her fiction and a sharp ring of truth. In *The Sweet Dove Died* she wrote closer to the bone of her own life than in any other previous novel. The first page was clearly set in Christie's and calls up the scene of thirty years ago. "... the dealers hunched over the table in their shabby clothes, making their bids with raised eyebrows or scarcely perceptible movements of hands or catalogues. The other bidders or spectators, mostly men, were crowded in rows or small chairs or standing in corners." Overcome with the heat and excitement, our heroine, Leonora, unlike Pym, swayed sideways at "her moment of triumph" and was promptly escorted from the auction by two gallant gentlemen. Humphrey and his good-looking nephew James, were both to become romantically inclined. Pym had jotted in her diary in June 1964: "Walking in Bond Street I see a young man sitting alone in a grand antique shop, presumably waiting for customers. A woman admirer might be a great nuisance, always coming to see him." Pym switched this cameo version for her novel, to the Sloane Square area, where Skipper had his antique shop L'Atelier. In *The Sweet Dove Died* we read: "A man sitting in a shop, perhaps especially in an antique shop, is in a vulnerable position. It had not occurred to James that Phoebe would ever come to London uninvited." The Jane Austen turn of phrase was another Pymian pastiche. She would introduce the odd line to usher in a favourite author. A second Austen simile adorned a visit to a cat show: "It is a truth now universally acknowledged that owners grow to look like their pets ..." A third comes to light: "To be involved with a man's furniture, especially to have some of it in one's possession, even if only temporarily, adds considerably to one's prestige ..." In a letter to Pym, from Larkin, while on a summer holiday in Sark: "I think autumn and winter are better than spring and summer in that they are not <u>supposed</u> to be enjoyable." An observation that clearly appealed to Pym who again recycled it in her novel. In an evening garden scene between Leonora and James, he admired the amethyst coloured dress she was wearing.

"It's autumnal, somehow."

"You mean that I look old? That I'm in the autumn of life?"

"You know that I didn't mean that! And anyway autumn is a much pleasanter season than spring or summer ..."

A further tart dialogue between Leonora and James suggests a parody on Ivy Compton-Burnett; Pym had always been influenced by her sparing style and her crisp dry humour. Leonora had persuaded the tentative and handsome James to stay to supper.

"One always has <u>something</u> – tins and packets and eggs, and things in the fridge."

"I expect people often drop in to see you."

"Yes, of course."

"You don't mind living alone, then?"

"No – otherwise I wouldn't."

Pym's evening at Covent Garden with Skipper was predictably resuscitated. But she lowered the romantic pressure by pairing Leonora with 'funny old Humphrey' rather than James: 'Leonora was looking beautiful and remote in black lace. "Such ravishing music," she whispered, leaning towards Humphrey and allowing his sleeve to brush against her bare arm.' Pym's visit to Keat's House was noted in her diary 14th August 1963. 'A wet day. Hampstead, Keat's House ... inside it is rather austere and simple.' It was revived as a sad little setting. Leonora and James and his nauseous new friend, Ned, made a disparate trio as they approached.

"We shan't be walking about outside," said James. "So there's no need for any of us to get wet." All the same, the overcast skies and dripping rain spread a pall of sadness over the little house, with its single bare rooms.

Pym's portrayal of Leonora's lovelorn dejection is a masterpiece. Propped in a café beside some man who was tackling a doughnut with his knife and fork was the last straw. Leonora shuddered. Wrote Pym: 'She turned her head away and huddled into her fur coat, feeling herself debased, diminished, crushed and trodden into the ground, indeed 'brought to a certain point of dilapidation'. "I am utterly alone," she thought.' To cheer and comfort her heroine, Pym next wheeled in Fortnum and Mason to alleviate the scene. 'She wanted to feel soft carpets under her feet and to move among jars of foie gras and bottles of peaches in brandy.' Gamages and Wimpy bars and Kardomah restaurants were more Pym's purlieus but for Leonora she had had to aim higher.

' "Taxi, Madam?" The doorman, solicitious as such people always were to Leonora, was holding an umbrella over her, for a few flakes of snow were beginning to fall.'

Pym had started her novel on Leonora with a degree of scepticism. She was originally planned as a minor character. But the novelty of developing a spoilt, manipulative creature finally to be lost in ignominy and pathos had intrigued Pym. Larkin, to whom she first sent her MS found *The Sweet Dove Died* sad and moving, with more feeling in the book than in any of her others. He advised "fewer characters and slower movement". Thanking Larkin for his trouble, she ended her letter, in October 1968: "I do hope you will get something better to read than unpublished, unpublishable novels!" Still apprehensive from her rebuffs and lacking her old confidence, Pym launched herself on her trek for a publisher. In August 1969, Longmans returned *The Sweet Dove Died*. She noted despairingly: "Longmans returned *The Sweet Dove* 'well written' – but what's the use of that ..." Constable assured her wanly that it was '... "virtually impossible" for a novel like *Sweet Dove* to be published now.' "My novel has had its umpteenth rejection (from Cassell)." And donning her smart white mackintosh, in her lunch hour from IAI, she retrieved her manuscript. "After lunch I go to Red Lion Square and enter the portals of Cassell's to collect the nicely done-up manuscript. Where next? Up to Faber in Queen's Square?" Should she experiment with her male pseudonym? "I shall call it *Leonora* by Tom Crampton and send it out again," she resolved, after yet another rejection from Macdonald. But Macmillan, destined to fête her in seven years time, further pronounced the book a commercial liability. In October 1970, Pym hoped she had been accepted by Peter Davies. There was fulsome praise from the directors: "very accomplished" … "a minor tour de force" and the snide comment: "clever-clever and decadent" – which Pym enjoyed "… that made me feel about thirty years younger!" Through the next few years, Pym was to approach 21 publishers.

14

Barbara and Ivy

Pym's fortunes were soon to be dashed, from another quarter. At the end of
April 1971 she had touched on a small lump in her left breast. Shocked and
with the added discomfort of Hilary away in Greece, she was whisked off to
St Mary's Hospital, Paddington. It was diagnosed malignant. Pym, in her
stoical acceptance of things adopted a fondness for her 'little lump'. She had
evolved any occurrence in her life to its own material value; bad occurrences
she aligned to tough meat that had to be minced, processed and re-created
into a written art form. Re-admitted to hospital the next day, she underwent
a mastectomy. Pym faced up cheerfully to her fate – everybody had been so
kind. Hazel Holt and friends from the IAI were a tower of strength, bringing
flowers and grapes and books. She was the centre of interest, to include the
avid gaze of students. "To have a lovely rest" was a rare novelty, and "the
black hands and the white hands, so cool and firm and comforting."

From her small ward in the aisle she soon strolled through to the main
ward in her search for 'material'. Talking and moving among the patients she
found any tentative enquiry led to a voluble life history. The gestation for
Quartet in Autumn was building up. How easily she could now impart –
perhaps to a woman in the office – a false breast. Convalescing in the garden
at Brooksville Avenue, and enjoying a spate of spring sunshine, she wrote to
Larkin: "Since there are no longer hushed voices when one speaks of it I'll
tell you that it was a breast cancer; luckily caught when very small so I hope
there won't be any recurrence, though I suppose one mustn't be over-
optimistic." She then recalled to him Penelope Mortimer, who in true
Pymian mode had devised her best-selling novel four years earlier *My Friend
says it's Bulletproof*. Being 25 years older, Pym felt more philosophical about
any loss of physical beauty. The fitting of her false breast even amused her

("A very fine shape indeed"). She returned to the IAI three months after her morbid revelation. Neither she nor Hilary had mentioned their mother's death from cancer. Pym's attitude was to forget any negative aspect; to move on, enriched with her senior material. ("… so unless anything unforeseen happens I am clear of that!") she wrote to a squeamish Larkin.

Nearing the end of another 'annus horribilis', her mind was full of plans; to pass her long eluded driving test, to publish another novel, even to write another novel. The following spring, the Pym sisters left Queen's Park for a new life near Oxford in the village of Finstock. Still employed at IAI, Pym spent the weeks in a bed-sitting room at 32 Balcombe Street, between Marylebone Road and Dorset Square. Thirty years on I was invited to see round this late Georgian terraced house. 'Andy' with a ravel of black hair cascading to his waist, occupied the ground floor. A band leader and guitarist, his gear to include three guitars, a variety of black boots, black jackets and heavy black coats ranged round the front room. We talked through faint wafts of incense as I admired his Siamese cat stretched languorously on the kingsize bed. Which room did Andy think had been Barbara's? She had described her 'hostess' as a 'charming, vague eccentric' who charged a rent of £5 a week. Andy blanched at the modest sum. Clearly that lady of the house had lived on the first floor with the pair of elegant front windows. … "Barbara lying in her bed could hear the station announcer from Marylebone," I volunteered. Ah! Andy steered me into a sizeable single room, adjoining his own bizarre parlour. And she had "use of kitchen …" Andy led me down the passage to the kitchen, that gave on to a small patio. Again we stood in Andy's bedroom which had clearly once been Barbara's. It was still Barbara's. Pale high walls with a pretty floriate cornice; a sash window looked out over trees to a London sky. "Sometimes I hear those noisy station announcers too," Andy assured me. And in this room of understated elegance, Pym had mapped out the four diffident characters, destined to triumph in her novel *Quartet in Autumn*. I left my young host with a copy of Larkin's piece on "The world of Barbara Pym". (And Tennyson's line came to mind: 'Let the great world spin for ever down the ringing grooves of change.')

Each Friday Hilary would drive to Charlbury to meet Pym's 5 o'clock train from Paddington. After thirty years of London homes and their respective careers, a tranquil village life was re-establishing itself. It was a busy life. The comfort of cats and cardigans and garden creepers were tempered with church commitments and the flower rota, the brass and coffee morning meetings with the Local History Society. There were walks in Wychwood Forest, through its clearings and ancient tumbled stones. They collected fire wood and noted dead birds, hedgehog and rabbit and other variable "bits and pieces" for Pym's zestful note books. And there were lovely evening rambles to the village of Wilcote with its simple St Peter's church. Pym cherished "the little grassy graveyard" with the haunted-looking old house overlooking the tombstones. Remains of a Roman settlement, as by Finstock and nearby Fawler, were spread around the area. Pym's last novel, *A Few Green Leaves* was motivated by this local landscape. ('Fawler', from the Anglo Saxon 'patterned floor', to suggest mosaic.)

And the sisters entertained: The novelist Gilbert Phelps and the young and sociable Paul Binding, who was yet to publish his first novel – *Harmonica's Bridegroom* (1984), and other neighbours, and friends from Oxford. With Pym's literary revival in 1977, there were to be many more distinguished writers and journalists descending on Barn Cottage. Pym had enjoyed incorporating food in her novels. It was a creative comfort; a conduit between author and reader. In her diaries she detailed even more succulent meals than in her novels. And how indulgent of her to go to the Wimpole Buttery after a visit to the dentist, to sink her teeth into a "delicious creamy cake tasting of walnuts". Once in a derisory context she and Hilary concocted a bilious looking lime green milk jelly. It was christened 'Maschler pudding' after Tom Maschler, her editor at Cape, who had turned down her seventh novel. The beautifully brindled 'Minerva' stole many a show in both the novels and diaries, in the culinary field. Her weakness for 'custard and fried tomato skins' served her well for 17 years. Pym's lunch invitations in her fêted Oxford days were noted with relish; towards the end of her life, the carefully planned lunch menu for Larkin, at Barn Cottage, balanced the delectable with restraint.

Reading was a prime pleasure in Pym's retirement. Brought up with the edict that only biographies and memoirs were suitable for the mornings, she now indulged in the occasional 'matinal' novel, preferably while still in bed. In her article "In Defence of the Novel" *The Times* 22.2.78), Pym roundly decried the notion that novels were trivial and quoted a director of The London School of Economics who argued that '… the young should read novels "to understand what life is about …" ' Of course there was nothing derogatory about actually *writing* a novel in the morning maintained Pym; for herself and most writers it was the best time. Ironically in her final years, she was reading even more than she had anticipated. The Romantic Novelists Association, had engaged her as a preliminary judge of the 1974 awards. She complained to Larkin that although they varied from the historical to the contemporary 'romantic', she found they lacked humour and irony. She settled back to her life-long favourites: Charlotte M Yonge, Ivy Compton-Burnett, Henry James and Harold Acton's *Memoirs of an Aesthete*. And Larkin's newly published *High Windows* – he had inscribed it to her – and Doris Lessing's *The Summer before the Dark* – "I must get on with <u>my</u> novel – austere and plain though it may be – and get a new small notebook." Ultimately it was to Jane Austen and Ivy Compton-Burnett she turned for inspiration.

'Her bookshelves are full of the novels of Ivy Compton-Burnett,' observed Caroline Moorehead in her piece for *The Times* – September 1977 – "How Barbara Pym was discovered after 16 years in the cold."

Hilary had once met this stern, legendary idol. She had been taken by Olivia Manning to a BBC party. She particularly remembered Compton-Burnett's hair. It had been styled like a grey pumpkin and she had worn a plain black dress … and a pendant. Anthony Powell had also retained a striking cameo. Writing of her in *The Spectator* at the time of her death (August 1969), how he had first seen her in a black tricorne hat, worn for the Oxford and Cambridge boat-race. "She looked formidably severe." Another instance even more indicative of her intimidating aura was given by Francis King. Meticulously on time for a tea party at her large and lugubrious flat in Cornwall Gardens, he rang the doorbell. "I hope I am not disturbing you," he called up genially. "Please cling to that hope," reverberated down the dictophone. Pym's own introduction to Compton-Burnett was not auspicious: "Read *More Women than Men* and saw no point in it – unreal people and not much of a story." (The head mistress – Josephine Napier – could surely be described as an unconscionable cold fish.) During her years at Oxford, in the thrall of the English poets, it had been Spenser, Milton and Beowulf who had commanded Pym's attention. Robert Liddell, a life-long devoté of Compton-Burnett was to write an endearing study of her and fellow writer, Elizabeth Taylor, in his book *Elizabeth and Ivy*. Pym preferring to immerse herself in the more familiar Yonge soon detected "some patches of Ivy dialogue". Yonge's *The Daisy Chain* she found "very Compton-Burnett and very sad". She next read Compton-Burnett's *A House and its Head* and agreed with Liddell that it was "remarkably fine – but oh, what inhuman restraint!" By 1940 she saw considerably more point in Compton-Burnett. She wrote to Liddell: "The influence of Miss Compton-Burnett is very powerful once it takes hold, isn't it?" She and Liddell and Harvey had taken to writing to each other in the sharp, dry Compton-Burnett idiom. To Liddell in Helsingfors, Pym had written from Oswestry in early 1938 on 'Friends and Relations':

"What do you think about Austria and Germany?" asked Aunt Helen.

"Well, I always like the Germans," said Barbara.

"Oh, Barbara, surely you do not like the Germans?" said Aunt Helen.

"The ones I have met have been very nice," said Barbara in a firm, level tone. "I have a friend in Dresden …"

"Ah, I expect it is a young man," said Aunt Helen in a triumphant tone, "that is what it is."

"Well, yes," said Barbara, "it is a young man, but that is not why …"

"Oh, Barbara, you surely would not marry a German?" persisted Aunt Helen.

"No, I have no intention of marrying a German," said Barbara firmly …

"You would have to live in Germany," continued Aunt Helen, "You would not be able to live in Oswestry".

The assembled old ladies next speculated on Barbara's age: "But Barbara, she is how old – eighteen?"

"Barbara is twenty four," said Mrs Pym in a clear, ringing tone.

"Yes, I am twenty four," said Barbara in a low mumbling tone.

There was further speculation on an old lady in the village: "I suppose she is dead now."

"No," said Barbara, "I saw her walking into the town yesterday."

To Harvey in June 1946, she wrote: 'My dear Henry, I have so much news that I had better just fling it at you in Compton-Burnett style.' She gave a clipped résumé of Hilary's separation from 'Sandy' Walton, their father's remarriage, her new job at IAI. She was now an anthropologist. She had little time to write novels ...

Liddell, not to be outdone, sent to Pym his evocative account of a teatime visit with Compton-Burnett in Cornwall Gardens. She had offered him "marge" and a cream cheese that she and her astringent companion, the English furniture expert, Margaret Jourdain, made from sour milk, hung up in bags. He was next handed some gherkin. "Tea still goes through all its stages," noted Liddell. "One really needs something solid," said Miss C-B.

"Home made plum jam? Not too sweet."

'Miss C-B has grown more solid in these years and is one of the few people who like the Peace better than the War.'

"Oh, it is so nice to have no bombs," she said, "I could not bear them."

Liddell wrote Dame Ivy Compton-Burnett's obituary for *The Times*. She was 85 years old. In his own erudite style he conveyed her character well, bestowing on her 'a happy eye for eccentricity'. The cadaverous cheek bones and deep set eyes shone out from many obituaries in the Press. Writers to include Raymond Mortimer, Anthony Powell, Alan Pryce-Jones, Christopher Sykes, Lettice Cooper, Pamela Hansford-Johnson, Rosamond Lehmann and Olivia Manning, flocked to her Memorial Meeting at Crosby Hall. Pym was to revel in concocting her own 'Compton-Burnett', icy truisms, that brittle banter, and those plain pronouncements. Often she would link them with an Austen turn of phrase. In her last novel *A Few Green Leaves* we read two such lines that reflect intrinsically on Pym's own ambivalence: "Even the happily married woman with a nice considerate husband and splendid children might still feel that something was lacking. If she'd given up a promising career for these domestic things – as a concert pianist or a TV personality or even a social worker ..."

Pym in her characteristic modesty always repudiated the comparison between Jane Austen and herself. Certainly, Lord David Cecil, Austen's biographer, and a dedicated critic of Pym's work, made no pertinent concessions on her behalf. From Pym's visit to Chawton in August 1969, with her friend Bob Smith, we have her Boswellian widely quoted diary entry: "I put my hand down on Jane's desk and bring it up covered with dust. Oh that some of her genius might rub off on me!" The writer A L Rowse, noted for his works on the Elizabethan age, confessed to his whimsical sobriquet of

Pym – "The Jane Austen de nos jours". But in his essay: 'Miss Pym and Miss Austen' – he made the cautionary point that their social perimeters were poles apart. Austen was from the fringes of the 18th Century aristocracy while Pym straddled a crumbling middle-class.

Lord David held that Austen's genius had evolved by her early teens; at twelve years she had left impetuous scribbles in the margin of Goldsmith's *History of England*. She devoured books, striding happily through Dr Samuel Johnson, Henry Fielding and Fanny Burney. Soon she was honed to the more social and domestic contours of her period and the whole comedy of manners. Pym, also a precocious reader, had had a 'coup de foudre' aged sixteen years, when she came to Aldous Huxley's poetic novel, *Crome Yellow*. It had been put aside for her at the Boots' Lending Library in Oswestry. Fifty years later when talking books with Lord David, he told Pym how reading Lytton Strachey's *Eminent Victorians* had inspired him to write – ("Just as I had been inspired by *Crome Yellow*"), declared Pym in her diary. Both Pym and Austen learnt most from their early reading of favourite authors. From their shape, form and dialogue they were both to be profoundly influenced. Lord David concluded that Austen's genius lay in her pervasive sense of comedy and in the shape of her narrative. In February 1952, when Pym had two bestsellers under her belt, we see a note to herself in a diary entry: "Read some of Jane Austen's last chapters and find out how she manages all the loose ends."

It is clear that Pym was an arch disciple in the School of Jane Austen. They had essential guidelines in common; the perimeters of their narrow ground – (Austen never travelled abroad) – their astute insight in to the human comedy and their comfortable hold on their chosen miniaturist art form. But Austen's world was serene and elegant, shut tight to the Napoleonic wars and the French Revolution. Pym's world was a landslide of post-war destructions. Austen, a lady of the gentry, chronicled the thriving social fashions of her times for posterity. Pym in a changing society, delineated the demise of the privileges and the traditions of her present. Pym's talent was clearly perfected by her close attentions to Austen. A natural affinity could also be deduced from their mutual acceptance of things and their respective limitations; their capacity to make the best of bad circumstances; their cheerful fortitude through their considerable long wait for publication.

In his obituary on Pym for The Royal Society of Literature, Lord David ended his piece: "Within her chosen limits she has satisfied, as very few writers of her time have done, the rival claims of life and art, has managed continuously to delight our literary sense while, at the same time, providing us with an acutely observed record of English life in her time."

In those few words, Lord David could equally be conveying Jane Austen.

Yet we could argue that our fond perception of Pym with her coup d'oeil focussed solely on the middle-classes is misconceived. Did Pym look back to Charles Dickens in her highlighting of the shaming slump in our social order and deference? In her last novels, such examples are deftly portrayed. As A L Rowse in his essay recalls, there are 'ambivalent implications' in such scenes as evoked by Pym. From the wild dirty woman yelling "Fuck off!" to Mr Olatunde and his enlightenment of Letty Crowe, Rowse asks the reader: "What would Miss Austen think of such goings on?" But unlike Dickens and his savage, shock-provoking revelations of Victorian social crimes, Pym's instances are rendered politically correct, with her subtle humour.

15

Darkness into Day

In May 1974, Pym wrote to Smith: "Things are going well for me and I am now able to write letters ..." A month before she had suffered a mild stroke due to a surfeit of calcium in the blood, inducing high blood pressure. It had all had a debilitating effect on her reading and writing, resulting in a month's stay at the Radcliffe. She had jotted in her note book: "Dr Burke examineed [*sic*] me (+ studdens) [*sic*] and suscepts [*sic*] excess of parathroughoid [*sic*] gland in the neck ... hopefully home cerca Wednesday." *sic* In June she was again in hospital to have a parathyroid gland removed. She was booked in at The Churchill, Oxford, in a mixed ward, and was looking forward to their renowned breakfast bacon.

Larkin's newly published *High Windows* was by her bedside; a volume of poems reflecting his disenchantment with old age and hospitals and life's oppressions; his compassion for the human condition and his escapist fantasies. It included his memorable line: "They fuck you up, your mum and dad ... ." Pym was flattered he had sent her a copy ... ("I wish I could be more worthy of the very kind inscription you put in the book!").

Her operation completed, Pym was advised by her doctor to retire. She returned to the office for a further four weeks and was dismayed by changes in the general management; notably the dismissal of other older members of staff. She busied herself with her familiar tribal indexes and bibliography. Her retirement lunch went well, with her favourite anthropologists invited; her doctor had warned her not to get too excited. With her cheque she bought a large topaz, set in a substantial gold ring: "Almost as big as an Edith Sitwell ring!" she reported delightedly to Smith.

A year later Pym was writing a typically sympathetic letter to Larkin, asking tenderly after his low spirits, and his non-desire to write. She ended with the tentative invitation: "It would be so nice if you ever did 'find yourself' in Oxford and we could meet and have lunch …" After their twelve years' correspondence, it was a momentous move forward. Three weeks later on April 15th, 1975 she wrote again: "Dear Philip, Thank you very much for your letter. I should like very much to meet you for lunch on 23rd April (Wednesday) and, all things considered, I think it would be best to meet in Oxford." She suggested the Randolph Hotel. How would he recognise her? He, of course, she would know immediately; formidably tall in a tweed jacket with heavy rimmed spectacles – but she? "I am tallish (5′ 8 1/2 in the old measurements) with darkish brown hair cut short. I shall probably be wearing a beige tweed suit or a Welsh tweed cape if colder. I shall be looking rather anxious." If they didn't fancy the Randolph they could of course try somewhere else … but the Randolph awaited them in all its grand Gothic Victoriana. Both Pym and Larkin were shy; Larkin had even suffered a bad stammer through to his early twenties; their meeting was undoubtedly fraught with anticipation as they rounded on the vaulted front portal and found their way through to the Pugin-esque splendour of the oyster bar. A ruddy faced extrovert, propping up the counter talked loudly and fulsomely at them and perhaps happily dispelled any initial qualms.

They were soon ushered to a table looking out on the Grecian grandiloquence of the Ashmolean. Sure of their ground, it was a delightful meeting. Larkin later referred to "that happy sunny day in Oxford which was so enjoyable". Their correspondence resumed immediately; he urged her to continue with her novel on impoverished retirement.

The following August, Pym was to have another unnerving experience. One Sunday morning she and Hilary strolled up through the village to Gilbert Phelp's cottage perched high on the East slope. The snug, deep-set windows and pointed wood porch looked inviting for the few friends asked along to a drink before lunch. Pym was suddenly distressed when, in the middle of a sentence, she could not remember the name of the currently much publicised, Dr Kissinger. She became tongue-tied and effectively dumb. It did not last long, but she was conscious of the concern around her. "I wasn't offered another glass of sherry but perhaps that was just coincidence!" she noted in her diary. Successive disorders did not escape her; notably pins and needles in her right hand and jagged images of flashing colour after watching television. Her doctor prescribed a strong dose of the beta-blocking drug, Propranolol. Curious to know of possible side effects, Pym took herself to the library: "nausea, diarrhoea, insomnia". She certainly conceded to feeling off colour. But then so did Jock with his eye operation and his grief over Elizabeth Taylor. Both Rupert Gleadow and Gordon Glover were dead and Henry had come to tea with a bad cold. Tom Boilkin, the cat, had died peacefully on a copy of *The Times*... Pym now resolved that any anxieties she had should be focussed on finishing her novel: *Four Point Turn*. Each six monthly check up at the Radcliffe loomed as a stern bid to complete.

By spring 1976, Pym was typing out her novel. She forwarded it to Larkin for his opinion. He was moved by the courage displayed by her ageing characters; "Marcia's battiness is splendidly caught." He felt the title *Four Point Turn* too abrupt for the compassion and the innuendo revealed. Might she change it for something sadder and more subdued? He also queried the sum total of her 48,000 words — should the book be longer? If only for commercial interests? He sent a typescript to Pamela Hansford Johnson, who promptly recommended the novel to Hamish Hamilton. He replied to say that he was "eager to read it", quite overlooking the fact that he had already rejected it. Pym recorded cynically in her note book: "The embarrassment of being an unpublished novelist knows no bounds and what price the memory of publishers!" Undaunted she continued to work on her novel and on Larkin's advice added more chapters; the select lunch party, accompanied by "Father G" after Marcia's funeral at the Crematorium, was an inspired addition. Father G, finding himself agreeably placed in a restaurant rather than squeezed into a suburban sitting room, badly fancied a dry martini, was it appropriate he wondered? Even the hesitant Letty was persuaded to sample one. "That will pull you together," Father G had assured her. She had to agree and the notion that they should not be drinking, with poor Marcia teetotal was soon swept aside. A drink was clearly a comfort at such times and Letty felt strangely encouraged to see her life in retirement as a renewed opportunity. Marcia's name was not mentioned until the pudding.

Pym's other commendable chapter to pad out the script took the churchy Edwin to a memorial service. It resulted in an appreciably long lunch hour from the office. In a church, admirably heated for a January morning, Edwin approved the smart assemblage of fur coats and hats and "dark-suited men in good, heavy overcoats". The stiff sprigs of holly, left over from Christmas were augmented by a generous show of white chrysanthemums on either side of the altar. But for Edwin, proceedings really came to life as the congregation filed out; he noticed that the initiated few were narrowly slipping through a side door into a vestry. Edwin peered further and glimpsed glasses of sherry laid out on a white cloth. He slipped through himself; after all, he looked suitably grey and sombre and nondescript. He was further gratified to find a choice of medium or dry or sweet sherry. He cast an eye over the vestry paraphernalia; candlesticks, "a discarded crucifix of elaborate design, probably condemned by the brass ladies as impossible to clean." A pristine white surplice hung from a hook on a hanger. Edwin noticed the elderly man beside him put down his empty glass and take another . . . . "He'd like to think of us here drinking sherry." A woman joined them . . . "Matthew never entered a church in his life, so perhaps the drinking would be all he'd approve of."

Pym had contrived this whole vestry scene from her own memory and diary entry of Daryll Forde's Thanksgiving Service at the London University Church in Gordon Square.

In a letter to Larkin:

11th July 1973
32 Balcombe Street

DF was <u>not</u> a believer so it wasn't very Christian though the Chaplain gave a kind of blessing at the end ... Afterwards some of us were invited to have a drink in what was described as an 'anteroom' but really it was a kind of vestry with crucifixes and hymnbooks lying around and, on a hanger, a very beautiful <u>white</u> cassock or soutane ... it was like something that I might have put into a novel ..."

Both these supplementary chapters indicate the ease in which Pym combines a dash of eccentricity with her humour. The vignettes stored in her head and in her note books from years before, delight with their reappearance in a novel. Her talent for light comedy is not demeaned by its facile flow.

The summer and autumn of 1976 passed happily and quietly for Pym and Hilary. Day outings to Oxford, country walks, pottering around churches and a visit from Larkin and his matronly companion, Monica Jones. Pym still busied herself with reading batches of 'romantic' novels. She found few that she liked, but admitted to her own increasing old age. Her thoughts turned to yet another novel. She wrote to Harvey, who had come to live in Worcestershire, some thirty miles away. "Novel writing is a kind of personal pleasure and satisfaction, even if nothing comes of it in worldly terms ... (? Is gardening enough. No!)" In May the sisters had spent a week in Greece. Pym, aghast, reported on the encroaching litter and the ubiquitous plastic carrier bag; dumped heedlessly in the sea, on the beach "and indeed everywhere". Even priests with white beards carried their plastic bag. Japanese cars were another aberration. In September they stayed with friends at Snape and pottered around Aldeburgh. "Full of refined-looking retired people." (Her comment suggests of more Agatha Christie potential than Pym.) Such halcyon days could have hardly presaged the dramatic turn that pitchforked Pym into a novel sensation.

Over a leisurely lunch in October 2002, Paul Binding, author and literary reviewer, lunched with me in Regent's Park and reminisced on Pym and Hilary. In the mid-1970's he had lived in a gold stone cottage near Finstock, in the village of Wroxton. He wrote Pym a fan letter and asked the two sisters to supper. Aged 30 years and working in Oxford for the Oxford University Press, he described himself then as a bashful young bachelor with no pretensions. It was Lord David Cecil, his former tutor, who had introduced him to Pym's writing. Binding had spent Christmases at Cranborne and had come to regard Lord David as a surrogate father.

As Binding waited tentatively for his two guests he was shocked to see them alight in full evening dress on to his muddy front yard. Was Pym beautifully dressed? Binding felt that Pym has been over glamourised. He personally found her socially awkward and badly dressed. She was clever, formidably well-informed and a shrewd observer. He looked on her essentially as a person rather than a woman. She was always friendly but undeniably 'éloignée'. Was she attractive to men? In his own capacity as a younger man had Binding judged her as asexual and virginal? "She made me feel that strong dividing line between men and women." But there was a special empathy between Pym and younger men? Undoubtedly, but Binding himself, a perennially handsome man had sensed no chemical attraction. Pym had been angry, he assured me, over her rejection. Not obsessively so but she would talk freely when the subject was raised. She believed intrinsically in her books and their ultimate merit. Binding detected a suppressed depressive side to Pym. He liked her best for elucidating the disappointments of life and for her perceptive lead through the daily round, to stave off melancholia.

Binding is proud that he was the first to break the news to Pym of her triumphant citation in the *Times Literary Supplement*. On Friday January 21st 1977 there was published an illustrated list compiled by the literati, of the most underrated and overrated writers of the century. Pym was named twice as a most underrated writer, by both Lord David and Larkin ... "and there was no collusion, as Philip afterwards told me!" she wrote gleefully to Bob Smith in Ibadan. Binding spotted the awards, at his desk at the OUP. Driving home through the cold wet night he was aware that the Pym sisters might not take the *TLS*. When he telephoned that evening from his cottage he asked Pym: "Do you take the *TLS*?" ... And Binding had the satisfaction of telling her: "There is something of great import for you." The next day it was on the front page of *The Times*.

It is indicative of Pym's attraction that her readers return again and again. They have their favourite books and less favourite books; some act as a curative, a restorative, and all can enhance the mood. Her friend, Bob Smith, has been widely quoted: "... Barbara Pym has been a provider of the very best sort of 'books for a bad day'". Binding told me that he had not enjoyed Pym's last novel *A Few Green Leaves*. He saw in her and her writing a reflection of the urban type rather than a country person. His favourite novel was *Less than Angels*; it is possibly the most popular of Pym's novels, involving youth and allusions to anthropology. And Binding pointed out that there were more men in the novel. He had relished the scene when the two male students had complied to take out the formidable Esther Clovis to lunch. She was portrayed by Pym: "... of stocky build with roughly cut short hair and tweedy clothes." Miss Clovis, with her provenance from a 'Learned

Society' was in nominal charge of the 'Research Grants'. Mark and Digby felt that an invitation out to lunch might ingratiate themselves to her. She accepted with alacrity and they were swept away with only one pound and three shillings between them. Miss Clovis had also scooped up her friend, Gertrude. Mark and Digby scoured the mercifully cheap menu and settled on braised tripe and macaroni cheese. They drank lemon squash assuring Miss Clovis that they never took anything stronger 'in the middle of the day'. Their two guests lashed into steak and chips and an assortment of vegetables for Miss Clovis, to include runner beans. She sipped voluptuously on her dark foaming Guinness. The pudding menu revealed jelly at 6d. 'Mark and Digby declared that they were passionately fond of jelly.' They eschewed coffee – ' "It might keep us awake in Dr Vere's lecture," joked Digby. He took out his pound note ... Miss Clovis pushed it back into his hand and snatched the bill from him.'

Friendships rooted in youth can come into play more fully in later years. Henry Harvey, now settled into a country retirement, again played a supportive role in Pym's last years. Divorced from his German, second wife, Susi, he pottered contentedly in his cottage with a large white cat for company. He had called it "Offa" after the powerful Anglo–Saxon ruler and builder of Offa's Dyke.

"Lunch with Henry in his nice cottage," recorded Pym in October 1977. She had found him unexpectedly domesticated, absorbed with jam making and tending his vegetable garden.

Three months later Harvey took Pym on a weekend jaunt to Ross-on-Wye. They stopped at Cheltenham to drink the mineral spring water at the Pump Room. "Salty, healthy-tasting water," noted Pym and was relieved when they repaired to a café for coffee and cream to take the taste away. A few miles on, at Deerhurst, Harvey had earmarked another stop at Odda's Chapel; rare and Anglo–Saxon, it is incongruously attached to a 16th Century timbered farmhouse. After a pub lunch in the Forest of Dean they walked through ancient oak and beech trees with glimpses of the River Wye. Finally arriving at their hotel at Ross-on-Wye, Harvey made them both a cup of tea in his room. Their long relationship had evolved into a comfortable companionship. But these halcyon days were numbered.

A few months later, Pym spent a summer weekend in Worcestershire, when Harvey's first wife, Elsie, was there too. "17–19 August … strange situation dating back over 40 years. A long walk up the hill in lovely country. Three elderly people walking – not together, but in a long line separately, Elsie stopping to pick flowers." Years later in a talk at the Pen Club, Harvey commented on Pym's diary entry. It was a prime example of her "little polishing"; her fondness for a dash of rue to give a hint of melancholy, or a presage. He explained that they had walked in single file because the path was so narrow. "What actually happened was secondary to her writing of it."

On 4th March 1979, a mere ten months before her death, Harvey was lunching at Barn Cottage. He was making plans to take Pym to Derbyshire for another "weekend break". Pym listed 'sensible shoes' in her note book and a reminder not to drink too much. Her health was in a precarious and terminal state. Three weeks later she and Harvey were sitting over a large dinner at the Maynard Arms in Grindleford. The restaurant had a reputation for fine food and Harvey had further endeared himself by impressing on the wine waiter that their bottle of Orvieto should not be *too* cold.

She may also have been gratified that she had featured in *his* diary. On 23rd March 1979 he wrote that he had picked her up at Finstock and driven her to Grindleford (Maynard Arms Hotel) via Towcester. Over the weekend they: "Drove round in Derbyshire and got lost in a huge colliery trying to find Newstead. We looked in other hotels to see what people were eating." Their own hotel was in the heart of the Peak District National Park with fine views of the Derbyshire hills; an ideal starting point for exploring the surrounding country.

They had lunched at Eastwood, in Nottinghamshire, on their way; the birthplace of D H Lawrence and the provenance of his first novel *The White Peacock*. His idyllic descriptions of farms and lakes and cottages studiously shield the reader from the all-encroaching coal-mining industry. Eastwood becomes 'Eberwich' and Moorgreen Reservoir becomes 'Nethermere' – as the most romantic stretch of water that charmed the lives of all who existed round its edge. For Harvey, whose life had been immersed in English literature and authors, these forays into the writer's world were a strong enthusiasm. Did he recall for Pym the lines from *The White Peacock*? – "It was a grey, dree afternoon. The wind drifted a clammy fog across the hills, and the roads were black and deep with mud. The trees in the wood slouched

114

sulkily. It was a day to be shut out and ignored if possible. I heaped up the fire, and went to draw the curtains and made perfect the room." Through the years, Pym had been enchanted by Harvey's reciting and reading aloud; from Shakespeare's Sonnets to Richard Dawkins' *River at Eden*. And did he confess to her how much he had relished her early letters? Years after her death he would reminisce: "She used to write to me in Finland, just before the war. The most amusing, hilarious letters – she had a kind of crazy streak which came out in those letters – very, very funny indeed. I burnt them unfortunately. I thought Stalin might get hold of them."

On the Saturday of that last weekend together, Harvey kept up the pace. "Good breakfast!" approved Pym. "Drove to Eyam, the plague village, then to Bakewell." She described the church, in its beautiful setting as "warm and fragrant (but not incense, perhaps furniture polish)". Returning home on Sunday morning, they drove first to Hassop, where Pym wandered happily through the early 19th Century Catholic Church – "Classical style". At the nearby Hassop Hall Hotel, they gazed tentatively through its front windows at the tables laid for lunch. Steeped in Domesday and Civil War connections, the converted Byronic stone façade suggested a most superior hotel. A coal fire blazed in the hall where display cabinets of silver, and fresh flower arrangements embellished the scene. A little intimidated by the grandiloquence, they decided to press on. Harvey wanted to find Newstead Abbey, the home of Lord Byron. And Pym – ("Had to find a public loo.") But Newstead, a romantic ruin of a home, inherited by Byron, along with his title, at the age of ten years, eluded them. Later, as they snacked on tea and sandwiches in a motorway café, Pym mused, "A whole new civilisation."

16

Annus Mirabilis

One of the more entertaining interviews to evolve from Pym's resurrection took place with Lord David Cecil. Filmed mid-summer in the garden at Barn Cottage, it was later transmitted by the late night programme on BBC television, October 21st 1977. Pym had in fact met Lord David and his wife, Rachel, a few weeks previously at their Dorset home. There had been lapsang tea, ginger cake and a lot of talk about 'writing'. Rachel had much enjoyed *No Fond Return of Love*. The daughter of Sir Desmond MacCarthy, the late drama critic, she herself also attained to literary talent. In her diary entry of May 19th, Pym had briefly noted, rather ambiguously, 'Tea with Lord David Cecil. A comfortable agreeable room with green walls and some nice portraits. They are so easy to talk to ...'

Seated at a small tea table and screened by boughs of orange blossom and a border thick with foxglove and white roses, Lord David launched delicately into his quarry. Pym, radiant in a bold printed blue and white tunic and navy silk shirt nervously fondled Minerva the cat, to stave her off the milk jug. Hilary's comments spring to mind: "Barbara was always rather shy. She was not a stutterer but she was hesitant. Never a great talker. She would not hold the floor at a dinner party." How would she acquit herself exposed to a vast unknown audience with this acclaimed literary figure? Lord David deftly unravelled Pym's precepts as he coaxed out her smiles and sidelong glances. Her shyness and modesty were an overt attraction to her audience who drew closer. Her voice and delivery was clear and measured with a pleasing lilt. As in her writing, there were no wasted words.

Lord David, slim and elegant in a light flannel suit introduced Pym as a novelist who wrote stories about quiet people. He affirmed that he himself read Pym with pleasure – that he liked life more when reading them and afterwards too. He had finally read all her novels, relishing their good-tempered absurdities, the comedies of life, devoid of all sentimentality. "A surprising variety of people like my novels," Pym assured him. "Women of my age, men also and younger men." Was she enjoying her retirement? Indeed, she found it extremely beneficial, with more time for writing and other things; the cooking and housework, dress-making, gardening, walking, church activities, coping with the cats and entertaining at tea ...

"My ideal pattern is to write in the morning... I write quite quickly. But ... it takes time to write a book." Lord David next asked Pym about her novel *Quartet in Autumn* to be published that autumn. It focussed on retirement and old age. Spry and silver-haired, in his seventy-fifth year, Lord David's interest might have been especially pertinent. "People make such a business of retiring," explained Pym. "My four characters, two men and two women, all in their early sixties were on the verge of retirement. I described their existing office life and then followed each one through the space of a year, with what happened to them." One woman had a mastectomy; a direct transference of Pym's own recent experience.

It was her own approaching retirement that had prompted Pym to write her well received *Quartet in Autumn*. In 1972–1974 she was offered a room in the house of friends at 32 Balcombe Street, leading off Dorset Square. Early in the morning, with the pampering inducement of breakfast in bed, she would make potted biographies of her four characters, before setting off to work. In a disconsolate letter to Philip Larkin, July 19th, 1974, she had referred to 'the manuscript of a novel I've started to write about older people working in an office. It's rather discouraging to go on writing with so little hope of publication but I try not to think about that.' (Three years later *Quartet in Autumn* was the runner-up to The Booker Prize.) And what novels did she read, Lord David finally wanted to know? "Jane Austen of course," answered Pym archly. (Lord David's notable biography *A Portrait of Jane Austen* was about to be published) – "Trollope and Elizabeth Taylor and the more modern Iris Murdoch. Ivy Compton-Burnett I admired and her dialogue influenced me."

But it was the Anglican Church centred on the village life of the established middle classes that was the crux of Pym's earlier novels. With a subtle eye she satirised the ambivalence of the great and the good; those pampered vicars with their handsome heads of hair; that marked predilection for their own voice; their unabashed leaning on wives and friends and their imperial immunity from any domestic interruptions. Pym's vicars, drawn invariably from her own past heroes, were cocooned and protected from the world. Her memorable Archdeacon founded on her life-long love, Henry Harvey, was the most peevish of them all. A scene is described in her first novel *Some Tame Gazelle* in which the Archdeacon calls out from his bedroom window that his wife has let the moth get into his best grey suit. The assembled women on the lawn below, making preparations for the garden party could only admire him. The heroine, Belinda Bede, (in effect, Barbara Pym), 'thought he looked so handsome in his dark green dressing gown with his hair all ruffled.'

Pym, a regular churchgoer all her life was always reticent over her innermost beliefs. She assured Lord David that she never strayed away. The Anglican Church gave a valid pattern to her life: "the buildings, the traditions and the music – I would not say more than that."

Next Lord David skimmed through her early curriculum. "You took a BA with honors at St Hilda's, Oxford."

"Yes, a second in English Literature. It was one of the best periods in my life ... and the chaperone rules were no solo visits to mens' rooms or on the river. In 1934 I started my first novel." (*Some Tame Gazelle* was based on her young Oxford friends, projected into staid middle age.) In her thirtieth year, in 1943, Pym joined the WRNS. Her subsequent years at the International African Institute were to prove a valid cornerstone for her writing career. She soon became assistant editor to their quarterly *Africa*. "I never went to Africa," she confessed to Lord David. "I met and talked with a lot of authors and anthropologists. I edited their articles and chose the review writers." Rather Africa had come to her, well filtered, and she selected her vignettes for her books accordingly.

"And I am interested in faceless, deprived people," Pym lowered her voice confidentially. Lord David nodded sagely. Continued Pym, "There is not much coverage in fiction. They are not popular heroes. Perhaps I think I am unsuccessful – hard to analyse what it is exactly ..."

Lord David switched to the subject of men. He suggested that she had a low opinion of the sex; that she treated her male characters in a derogatory way. Did she find them vain and self-centred? Ineffectual? "That is certainly not my view of men in general!" retorted Pym. She later wrote to Larkin, how she had quickly to suppress her exclamation, "Oh, but I LOVE men!" Pym swung back the conversation to her more preferred notions. "I like to observe people; odd people. I accept strangeness. I am a loner myself. I like solitude, being detached from things." She continued in ebullient vein, smiling coquettishly at Lord David: "And I like tea parties, dinner parties, church sandwich parties and even disastrous parties." She explained, "Parties are fruitful sources of disaster. There is always an element of disaster in a party."

It had been an exacting day. Larkin wrote congratulating her on her 'cool' and her 'pretty and luxuriant garden'. That same morning, Will Wyatt, Producer of the BBC Book Programme, had interviewed Pym in the churchyard. Walking up the hill from the cottage she had stood with her back to the church door. Looking exceptionally young and glowing, with no hint of her approaching death, she recalled her Shropshire childhood. The social axis had revolved around the church. "There were always two or three curates to ask to supper. Today the church cannot afford all that clergy." She had found the va et vient of church activity a good lead for fiction. Her interviewer appeared sceptical. When did she think up her novels? "Oh, ideas come all the time." She added meaningfully, "At this very minute something might be germinating." Her interviewer looked distinctly abashed: "Meeting people, doing housework, washing up, lunch hours at the Kardomah in Fetter Lane were always a fruitful source of ideas." (At The Restful Tray in Lower Regent Street, she and her colleague had once seen a nun tucking into steak on Ash Wednesday.)

Lord David's allusion to 'the small blameless comforts' of everyday life, depicted in Pym's early novels, was outmoded by her later work. Her themes had darkened. Her observations of the emerging squalid disorders had adopted a new cutting edge. Vandalism in churches, schools and public parks and the infiltration of alien cultures, filthy language and the wholesome tolerance for homosexual pairings; most of all the tidal wave of destruction to the middle classes. Pym's highlighting of such social and urban decay was achieved with her sense of comedy unimpaired. The confrontation of Letty and her Nigerian landlord (*Quartet in Autumn*) comes to mind. How could she, a daughter of respectable, middle class parents end up surrounded by Nigerians singing their heads off? Letty taps timidly on their door and complains of the noise which she finds disturbing. "Christianity IS disturbing," agrees her ingratiating neighbour. Mr Olatunde's reply is as profound as it is comic. It is pure Pym. Another churchy hero, Edwin, is on an evening walk. He stops to study the church notice board but when he turns the door handle he finds it locked. A pity, but that was the way things were now. It was wasn't safe to leave a church open, what with thefts and vandalism. (And he abhorred all talk of guitars at Evening Service, standing up to pray and shaking hands with the person next to you …)

Letty makes a collection of 'upsetting' sights. That woman slumped on a seat in the Underground reminded her fearfully of an old school friend. "Ought one to DO something?" – "Fuck off!" yelled the woman when disturbed by a kind, young girl. Letty is relieved that it is not her friend of 50 years ago. "Janet would never have used such an expression." Norman, a fellow member of the 'Quartet' has a secret penchant for muttering "Bugger, bugger, bugger". Nobody ever hears him. And Marcia, the fourth link, finds 'KILL ASIAN SHIT' scrawled across the wall of her station platform. 'She stared at the inscription and mouthed the words to herself as if considering their implication.'

Such urban profanities were still not so voracious or violating in the 1970's. In her bid to update her cosier cameos of the quiet life, Pym had probed alien fields. Her vignettes of dirt, crime and flagrant disrespect had been twisted into gentle comedy; that her examples of opprobrium needed society's consideration and care was implicit.

It was in this, her penultimate novel, *Quartet in Autumn* – that Pym had probed the perplexities of old age; its deprivations and loneliness. Indeed loneliness was the salient theme, countered by that staunch lack of self-pity. Marcia, an ambivalent study of hilarity and despair, exudes eccentricity, with her obsession for hoarding empty milk bottles and the gloating in her cupboard of tinned foods; she never disturbed them, preferring instead to open a small tin of pilchards from Snowy, the cat's own store. 'Marcia gave no thought to her own lunch and it was evening before she had anything to eat and then only a cup of tea and the remains of one of the bits of bread she found in the bread bin. She did not notice the greenish mould fringing the crust, but she wasn't hungry anyway and only ate half the slice, putting the remainder back for future consumption.'

Pym earmarked Christmas Day as the nadir for single people. Remorseless, tyrannical, there was no mistaking that day. It had to be coaxed along and survived. For Letty, it was not the conspicuous loneliness of cooking a chicken for one that upset, but that people might find out and pity her. As she sagely concluded: 'Still, Christmas Day had been lived through and was now nearly over, that was the main thing.' Marcia did not concern herself with Christmas any more. Now that her mother who would cook 'a nice capon' had gone and Snowy also, there was no point to Christmas Day. It just merged into other days. Such bleak disclaimers must ring true for many. In a letter to Philip Larkin January 12th 1964, Pym wrote tentatively: 'I hope you survived Christmas – we had four people staying for part of the time, and it is a rather exhausting ordeal for the churchgoer ...' Knowing that he had spent the days alone she made little of their festivities.

Quartet in Autumn after protracted rejections was finally published by Macmillan in September 1977, and directly attributed to the dramatic volteface of her literary fortune. In the *Times Literary Supplement* of January 21st, Lord David had been quoted: "Barbara Pym, whose unpretentious, subtle, accomplished novels, especially *Excellent Women* and *A Glass of Blessings* are for me the finest examples of high comedy to have appeared in England during the past seventy five years." Philip Larkin had qualified: "Underrated: the six novels of Barbara Pym published between 1950 and 1961 which give an unrivalled picture of a small section of middle class post war England. She has a unique eye and ear for the small poignancies and comedies of everyday life."

With her reputation so spectacularly revived, Pym was swept up in a flurry of media attention. There were requests for interviews and broadcasts and plans for a serial reading of *Quartet in Autumn*. Tom Maschler wrote to her cajolingly from Cape and mused on the telephone with Alan Maclean of Macmillan. Cape had to content itself with issuing reprints of the previous novels. An astringent interview with Pamela Howe, the BBC producer, had taken place on August 17th at the Bristol studios. An appallingly wet day with thunder and floods resulted in Pym and Howe muddling their umbrellas only to be discovered miles apart. Pym saw in it an episode for a story; the chagrin, the irritation ... and who got the inferior umbrella?

Howe admitted freely to Pym that she had not heard of her before the revelations of the *TLS* panel. Replied Pym gamely: "Every writer wants to be discovered – but rediscovery! I though it might happen when I was dead. I had begun to give up hope. I had been so discouraged." She explained how her novels had developed from her long career at the IAI. It was informative work and had influenced her to observe people observing other people. Village life, library life, church life, and the life of anthropology formed the structures of her earlier books, with her chronic observation at the core. "This perception of ordinary peoples' behaviour – you don't find it unnerving at times to observe so consciously?" Howe sounded perplexed. She next touched on Pym's idiosyncratic portrayal of men: "You exhibit an assured tolerance of men's frailties ... you are widely and subtly very much more destructive of men than the shrill women's libbers."

"That is not my attitude at all," protested Pym ... "But I don't like softness in people. I like people to have a certain hardness about them – an irony and detachment. If you are fond of people and of the church and I am very fond of the Anglican Church, then I think you can make fun of them."

Pym's *Four Point Turn – Last Quartet* – to finally evolve as *Quartet in Autumn* came as a shock to her more seasonal readers. That chill of death and loneliness; the fear of going dotty and dirty. What had become of those soothing cosy books at bedtime? But *Quartet in Autumn* was the critics' pet. Francis Wyndham in his intuitive review "The Gentle Power of Barbara Pym" for *The Sunday Times* 18.9.77 suggested: "Perhaps the subtlest thing about this quietly powerful book is her understanding of the obstinacy with which the individual will, continues to assert itself, even in situations bordering on desperate extremity." In this novel, Pym had 'come out' wrote Victoria Glendinning, in *The New York Times*. Headed 'The Best High Comedy', Glendinning set out her stall: "Letty ... trim, controlled and devout; Marcia teeters on the edge of dottiness using the public library shelves during the lunch hour as a place to dump her household rubbish." Their respective retirement was analysed by Glendinning: "Inner chaos threatens both. Letty does not let down her defences, and battles alone to preserve her sense of order and decency. Marcia, on the other hand, gives in entirely to her obsessions, hoarding plastic bags, and old newspapers and milk bottles in her dirty house, eating nothing at all and finally dying." Pym had scraped the barrel of all our ultimate dread. In depicting characters who appeared emotionally and domestically deprived, Pym had turned circumstances on its head. In the deadening cul-de-sacs of their losses we perceived that dogged pride of their survival. The validity of 'not having' was another notion of Pym's. Glendinning ended her piece: "It is in the ironic exploration of the "experience of not having" that Barbara Pym's art and originality lie."

Quartet in Autumn the book Pym wrote to keep her hand in; a page each early morning before work, was finally published on September 15th 1977. Pym wrote to Larkin from Barn Cottage on publication day + 1 – 16.9.77: 'I had a marvellous day – lovely weather and plenty of drink and even a telegram from James Wright in Macmillan. And of course the day before, articles in *Times* and *Guardian* by those clever young women.' (She preferred the *Guardian* article by Lesley Adamson.) She added that she had been making plum jam and would soon start on (green) tomato chutney. She had been stirring hard when James Wright rang to congratulate her on the *Times* and *Guardian* articles and feared she might have sounded 'distant'.

Concluded Lesley Adamson in her favoured article 'Guardian Women' ... "Barbara Pym isn't a fantasy person. She has always found enough to write about in life as it is lived around her. Her skill is pointing out the jokes that make up our lives, the comic possibilities we are too near-sighted to see.' Pym's second chronicler was Caroline Moorehead of *The Times*. The first paragraph set the scene for mild controversy. Pym's *Quartet in Autumn* could not be a best-seller; this miniature world of self-effacing suburbia was not to the taste of today's readership who were inured more to Edna O'Brien. Moorehead next visited Pym and Hilary at Barn Cottage. She reported: 'She is very much alive, a tall somewhat gawky woman.' She sympathised with Pym's publisher who perceived her heroines 'too pale for the bustling sixties, no match for the brilliance and anguish of Doris Lessing and Margaret Drabble women.' But slowly warming to the theme of the less the more, Moorehead heaved to Pym's modest satisfactions and the realisation that true pleasures are gleaned from small things. As though progressing to a higher grade of Pymian perception, Moorehead confessed sagely: 'Solace is to be found in food, clean linen sheets, a good deed knowingly performed.' The reviews were serious and good. "An Exquisite, even Magnificent Work of Art" – "An Important Novelist" – "The Wit and Style of a Twentieth Century Jane Austen".

Penelope Lively in her essay from the *Life and Work of Barbara Pym* edited by Dale Salwak; judged *Quartet in Autumn* – 'distinct from the rest and perhaps the finest achievement.' Pym's life long mentor and critic, Robert Liddell in his essay 'Success Story' termed it 'her most original and strongest novel'. Liddell's novelist friend, Francis King, who, incidentally, had found *Quartet in Autumn* profoundly sad and depressing, talked with the ageing author in 1991 at his flat in Athens. How would he now rate his four close friends, the most interesting of novelists: Ivy Compton-Burnett, Elizabeth Taylor, Olivia Manning and Barbara Pym? "Ivy was a genius, Elizabeth was a gifted artist, Olivia and Barbara were story-tellers who wrote well." The succinct answer surprised King who later commented: 'One can also imagine Barbara Pym being furious at it.' Their mutual friend Robert Smith in an article written in 1994 for *Twentieth Century Literature*, was indignant at Liddell's 'belittling estimate'. "I am not expecting a Pym resurrection." Liddell further wrote to him. Yet he had praised her *Quartet in Autumn* for its development and style. "And I think you are brave and clever to beat at this new track … the same and yet not the same." He again referred to *Quartet in Autumn* in his critical survey of Pym: "*Mind at Ease* published nine years after her death. "*Quartet* is darker and sadder than any other of Barbara's novels – it was begun after her first cancer operation – but it is her strongest, finest work."

In October 1977, *Quartet in Autumn* was short-listed for the Booker Prize. Tucked into her recently acquired fan mail – some from admirers who had thought she was dead – Pym received an invitation to the dinner to be held at Claridges on November 23rd: "… a once-in-a-lifetime opportunity to mingle in the 'Literary World'. Perhaps even to catch a glimpse of Maschler!"

17

The Fêted Fields

On February 29th 1992, James Runcie, film maker and writer, transmitted on television, a pastiche of Pym's passage to the Booker Prize dinner, held on November 23rd 1977. The live inclusion to the cast of her sister Hilary and Henry Harvey, with the actor David King as Larkin, and Mary Wimbush and Susan Wooldridge, added special dimension. Who could not be fascinated to see the real Henry? The unsurpassable Archdeacon Hoccleve? The script for *Miss Pym's Day Out*, takes 'Pym' portrayed by Patricia Routledge, through a jam-packed agenda. A frosty morning ride on her bicycle to a service at Finstock church, leads to the arrival of Henry at Barn Cottage with a bunch of blue iris: "To wish you luck. Not that I think you need it – I am sure you will win." Wrapped in tweed and a wool scarf – lean and handsome with a head of curling grey hair escaping from his floppy hat, he is magnanimous with pride and long affection. 'Pym' leaves him with Hilary as she goes to find a vase. "Barbara has a very heavy day ahead," warns Hilary. 'Pym' pauses as she arranges her flowers: 'An idea for a novel – a hopeless love for a man – when she's free she feels nothing for him. Is this the reward of virtue, this 'nothingness', or an enviable calm?'

Next we are jollied along to the village bazaar and even Pym had admitted her jaded interest in such events at the end of her life. But Jilly Cooper herself bounds up to her in a flurry of leonine hair: "Excuse me – are you Barbara Pym? I am a fantastic fan of yours – I love your books – I want to wish you luck for the Booker Prize." A mid-morning train now whisks us to London, for 'Pym's' appointment with her doctor. He has a talent to convey bad news nicely. And in an empty church nearby, 'Pym' prays aloud: "Preserve and continue this sick member in the unity of the church. Consider her contribution accepted." On to see Hazel Holt at the IAI. Ever immaculate and cheerful, she chats vivaciously crammed into her little room. Next Pym finds herself in a café for a well deserved cup of tea. She observes a dominant woman complaining to a "Mildred" or a "Belinda" about the danger of birds: "an owl bit a woman" – in the press the other day – and "swan knocks girl off bicycle" – the parks smothered in pigeons. Better to die in one's 60's – without being disabled." Patricia Routledge, who throughout the day, with her eloquent brown eyes, has conveyed Pym admirably, now takes herself and her charge to a hairdresser.

Runcie's subsequent scenario enacted in the grandiose ballroom of Claridges is well construed. A coterie of top publishers shuffle their feet uncomfortably at the memory of Pym's rejection over her seventh novel – *An Unsuitable Attachment*. A keen young advocate of her work, A N Wilson, leads the hue and cry ... "Yes, they should have read it ... but there was so much evidence against it ... reports from eminent readers considered it absolutely hopeless ... publishers get it into their heads that a particular style of writing is no longer fashionable ..."

In the actual event Pym relished her grand night out; from the roaring fire in Claridge's entrance hall ('those people sitting around – exiled Royals?') to the white and gold spaciousness of the ballroom to her swiftly handed gin and tonic. She was introduced to Lettice Cooper and to Penelope Lively and "Tom Maschler! (charming, of course)". At dinner she sat next to Ion Trewin, Literary Editor of *The Times*, and opposite Francis King, whose novels she admired. She was pleased with her outfit; a long, black pleated skirt and a "black blouse, Indian with painted flowers (C&A £4.90) and green beads". A photograph of her holding a leather bound runners' up copy of her book suggests an author in her prime.

Larkin had made a speech, divulging what the judges look for in the novels. Readability; credibility and ... "Did it move me?" He classed the two books of Pym and Caroline Blackwood "near misses" and pronounced the terminally ill Paul Scott, the winner. Scott's short novel – *Staying On* was the poignant portrait of an ageing couple choosing to live in India after 'independence'. The story was further immortalised by Celia Johnson and Trevor Howard for Granada Television. Larkin, in reply to Pym's effusive congratulations on his speech, confessed to her that he found "Bookernacht bewildering".

Runcie has our heroine take the train home alone; where Hilary is seen putting out the milk bottles, having heard the news on the radio, as she sat waiting by the fire. We are shown a neighbour in a pink fluffy dressing gown, sipping a milky drink. Beside her a vase of tired yellow November roses calls up the phrase "A few green leaves makes such a difference."

'Pym' arrives home at the moonlit garden gate, fresh, trim and seemingly unfazed by her momentous exertions. Propped up in the peace of her pillows and her virginal pastel lingerie, she now thinks on Larkin's new poem on death – "Aubade". She reads it often, with increasing pleasure: '. . . yet the dread of dying flashes afresh to hold and horrify – the total emptiness forever – not to be here not to be anywhere – nothing more terrible . . .' My "In-a-funk-about-death-poem" he calls it – she smiles and slips into sleep.

The Sweet Dove Died was ultimately published in June 1978, just nine months after the best-selling, severe and sobering *Quartet in Autumn*. Francis King reviewing for *Books and Bookman*, described the novel "like going out of a curtained sick-room into a sunlit garden". The steely sophistication of Leonora, her cum-uppance from a seasoned homosexual who usurps her idolised James, is pure theatre. King referred to the "sprightliness" in her writing and ended: "It is good to see Barbara Pym not merely back in print but triumphantly back in form." He openly preferred *The Sweet Dove Died* to her *Quartet in Autumn*. Susannah Clapp in the *Times Literary Supplement* (July 7th 1978) was quick to point out that Leonora's 'coolness' was indicative of the more modern 'phenomena'; "Leonora is not likeable." The fleeting glimpses of a handsome clergyman drinking tea on a train and a woman in a mackintosh pixie-hood at Keats House were nostalgic flash backs, suggested Clapp, to Pym's early novels. But it was Leonora, the new cool woman with her 'telling way with scarves and scent' who called the tunes in 'this graceful novel'. Peter Ackroyd in *The Sunday Times* (July 16th 1978) was less intrigued. He found Pym's world and characters locked in a bourgeoisie that rendered them immobile. He made a fanciful comparison of Pym's portrayal of homosexuality to "a peculiarly fruity aftershave: sensed but never discussed". 23rd September: "Hooray! The Sweet Dove is no 3 in the Sunday Times Best Sellers List." – a jubilant note in the author's diary.

Letters homed in from her faithful devotés. Larkin, delighted that she had heeded his revisions, admired her dexterity in turning the reader's dislike of Leonora into empathy. "And notable additions to your gallery of male monsters, though James is really too feeble to be called a monster." Lord David Cecil had appreciated Pym's pursuit of Leonora's dichotomous character. "Leonora is particularly brilliantly evoked." Bob Smith, from Nigeria, wrote in pragmatic vein: "People do seem to be getting your message these days. Perhaps this is what will distinguish the 1970s from those, in so many respects, brutal 1960s." And Richard Roberts? The amalgamated hero? What was his verdict? He had sent a card to Pym from Indonesia. "Well, rather wisely he didn't make much comment except to say how much he had enjoyed it. It was all such a long time ago anyway . . ." she wrote to 'Dearest Bob'.

Pym did not rest on her laurels. Her last book was centred on the Cotswold village of Finstock, where she and Hilary had lived in mutual content for seven years. "My next, if it ever gets finished, will probably be a let down for everyone – a dull village novel, with no bi- or homo-sexuality," she wrote wryly to Larkin. *A Few Green Leaves* – "my country novel" – was finished three months before her death. "It is a consoling book, an epilogue to her work . . ." wrote Robert Liddell in *A Mind at Ease*. He looked on *A Few Green Leaves* as "Barbara's farewell to her readers".

By March 1979, Pym's earlier novels were being re-issued by Cape. In New York, the publisher E P Dutton was following suit. Pym wrote to Larkin: "I have had super American reviews for *EW* and *Quartet in Autumn* including a long one in the *New Yorker* from John Updike (did you ever read *Couples?*)." Updike confessed he found it hard to assimilate the timid world of *Excellent Women* but recognised in Pym's novel *Quartet in Autumn*, written 25 years later, a style that was 'stronger, sadder, funnier, bolder'. He continued: 'The shadow of religious shelter has been lifted from Miss Pym's world, and the comedy is harder.' Updike was reminded of both Muriel Spark's *Memento Mori* and of Rose Macaulay's idiosyncratic *Towers of Trebizond*. Though he admitted he could not compare Pym's habitually quiet cast with the sophisticated and decadent eccentrics of Macaulay's. He likened Pym more to Larkin's world – 'the grey middle-class of an empireless England'. Updike, an essentially libidinous being was also bothered by the 'strikingly modest sex drives' in Pym's characters. Was she being modern or old-fashioned he pondered? Was she even predicting the demise of pro-creation in the face of ultra urban crowding?

'Out of the Swim with Barbara Pym' is a reappraisal by Isa Kapp; a regular book reviewer for *The New Leader*, whose work appears in *The Washington Post* and *The New Republic*. In 2001, 24 years after the publication of *Quartet in Autumn*, Kapp refers to the novel as 'the small masterpiece'. Pym's young protagonist reviews the spinal strength and detachment of her style; that attitude of self-sufficiency in women, their resource, their infinite capacity to eke a lot out of little, their pragmatic acceptance of things. Woman's superiority over man? Kapp insists that Pym was no feminist, but 'a great morale booster for women'. Pym was fundamentally a realist. She was no escapist. "It's up to oneself, to adapt to circumstances," reminded her resolute heroine, Letty. And, "Love was rather a terrible thing," decided Mildred, in *Excellent Women*. "Let other people 'get married'," her friend had advised. Kapp revives the scene in *The Sweet Dove Died* when Barbara Pym makes the first attempt in her fiction to bring her characters to the point of physical sex. That point, when James finds himself in Phoebe's cottage bedroom – 'standing in the little room, which had a sloping ceiling and walls patterned with wisteria, James put his arm round her shoulders, thinking that she was just a little too tall for him. He kissed her and after a few murmured endearments things happened so quickly that he could not afterwards have said who had taken the initiative.' On a successive visit James felt that 'making love to her was like an amusing unreal game, so far removed from his everyday life that he could not feel his usual guilt.' Pym herself soon tires of these scenarios and evokes with relish Phoebe's dirty kitchen; unwashed plates, unrinsed milk bottles and 'a bowl of lettuce from which he (James) surreptitiously removed a few inedible-looking leaves which seemed to have earth adhering to them.' There is nothing like a douche of comedy to put a dampener on sex.

Pym was next approached by the actress and writer, Beryl Bainbridge, who had just initiated a radio talk series: *Finding a Voice*. Writers were invited to make solo broadcasts on the approaches to their work. Pym's own successful recording was transmitted on April 4th 1978. "I rather dread hearing it as I don't like my voice but maybe I'll get used to it. Such is 'Fame', as you must know," she wrote coyly to Larkin.

"Is one's own voice a genetic or physical attribute? Or is it acquired deliberately?" In clear measured tones, Pym launched herself into her story.

As a schoolgirl she wrote for the school magazine and made parodies of favourite writers and their styles. She found Huxley's *Crome Yellow* the ultimate in sophisication. "It immediately attracted me." She liked detail; the makes of cars and cocktails and the descriptions of clothes. At Oxford she wrote a love story but tore it up. "Memory is a great transformer of pain into amusement," she could assure her listeners with a seasoned hindsight. It was to Betjeman and his *Continual Dew* that she had turned in her Oxford days. Betjeman and his "glorifying of ordinary things", of buildings and churches, seemed the quintessence of Oxford in the 1930's. She was influenced by Ivy Compton-Burnett: "But that precise and formal conversation seemed so stilted when I first read it." She read Stevie Smith's *Novel on Yellow Paper* and was struck by the human pathos. Lastly, from Jane Austen, she learnt the economy of language and the detachment of an author from her characters. "My own literary style was fashioned by those writers." She had found writing her first three novels comparatively easy; a mixture of all the worlds she knew about. "It's all inside you – then it becomes more difficult." There was a discernible pause in her delivery.

"In the early 1960's," she resumed, "to my horror, my seventh novel was rejected. 'Fiction lists full up for the next two years' I was told. Two subsequent novels were returned with the tags 'very well written' – 'too old-fashioned'. It was an awful humiliating sensation to be rejected. The swinging 60's had swung me out of fashion." Why do we write at all?, she wondered. Is it enough just to write for ourselves? She quoted her mentor Compton-Burnett: "Most of the pleasure would go if I felt nobody would share my book. But I would write for a dozen."

Pym next divulged that she was fascinated by the note books of great writers; Thomas Hardy's especially. She recited his small entry for October 25th 1867:

An old maid whose lover died
has his love letters to her bound and keeps
them on the parlour table.

She was also highly amused by Flaubert, who on going to a funeral had jotted in his note book: "Perhaps I shall get something for my Bovary."

Pym ended her solo address on a notion close to her heart. She recalled a favourite TV quiz game in which the panellists were asked to guess which author has written which passage. "I think that's the kind of immortality most authors would want – to feel that their work would be immediately recognisable as having been written by them and by nobody else."

On Friday April 7th, three days after her radio broadcast, Pym had a 'nasty turn'. She and Hilary were on their way to lunch at Abingdon when she suddenly felt faint and lost consciousness. She was taken by ambulance to the Radcliffe and soon came round to concerned doctors and juniors standing over her bed. No food and a night under observation was prescribed. She was allowed home the next day and told to return in two days. On the following Tuesday she had an ambulatory electro-cardiogram attached for 24 hours. "Took it off and returned it on Wednesday but have heard nothing. Am taking it easy and have written nothing for over a week." Pym was typically dismissive in her diary. Two weeks later her doctor was extolling the advantages of a pacemaker, which could be fitted to the heart. He also warned her that it should be removed on death – "as it is liable to explode in the Crematorium". Noted Pym in her diary ("He said I could use it in a book.")

A month later she was caught up in the triumphs of *The Sweet Dove Died* and discussing her Desert Island Discs with Roy Plomley, over cold salmon at the Lansdowne Club.

"Barbara Mary Crampton Pym – novelist and Fellow of the Royal Society of Literature, born June 2nd 1913." Roy Plomley, whose ingenious conception *Desert Island Discs* was first broadcast January 29th 1942, introduces Pym on to his programme, Saturday July 29th 1978.

"The first thing a novelist must provide is a separate world." Perhaps mindful of Larkin's words, Pym consciously wills herself on to her desert island. Chatting with Plomley she brings back the island again and again to central stage.

"Is music important to you?"

"I do like certain kinds of music. I have no musical skills. I could never play the piano well at school. I sang in the Bach choir at Oxford. I love singing about the house – the pop songs of my time – and on the island, I am sure." Her first choice … is the waltz at the end of Act II of Richard

Strauss' *Der Rosenkavalier*. The favourite tune of the crude and disreputable Baron Ochs; Pym found it "so invigorating and cheerful".

"Did you have a scheme in choosing the eight?"

"No – just things I really like." Her second choice is from Mozart's *Don Giovanni*: a piano variation by Chopin. "Là ci darem la mano" – (you'll lay your hand in mine dear). Pym liked the brilliant piano playing. "Again it is invigorating."

"Were you a bookish school girl?"

"I was fond of thrillers – Edgar Wallace was a favourite. In my mid-teens I turned to poetry."

Plomley puts her through her literary paces.

"Which writers made an early impression?"

"The first was Aldous Huxley with *Crome Yellow*. I was sixteen when I wrote and FINISHED the 267 hand written pages of *Young Men in Fancy Dress*. Quite an achievement. I never submitted it and never did anything with it. At Oxford I hardly wrote – I was too busy enjoying life – and working fairly hard at my English degree. When I came down from Oxford I tried to write a novel – at home. To sit at home trying to write was discouraging."

The war came and she joined the WRNS. She was stationed for some time at the agreeable neo-Palladian Exbury House located near the censorship offices in Southampton. Pym recalls "this vast area of the New Forest – of untrammelled heath and bog and woodland". She was next posted to Naples: "Checking out sailors' letters and that sort of thing. At the San Carlo opera house, I heard *Tosca* for the first time. Her third choice, from Puccini's *Tosca*, is 'Vissi d'arte, vissi d'amore" – Tosca's moving prayer for the safe reprieve from death of her lover, Cavaradossi.

After the war, in 1946, Pym was offered a job at the IAI. She worked in the editorial department, promoting research into African Cultures and languages. In 1948 she took up writing again. "Writing gets a hold of you in a curious way. I couldn't really leave it alone." In 1950 her first novel – begun in 1939 – was published by Cape.

"Were you never tempted to be a full time writer?" asks Plomley.

"Not seriously. I haven't got the temperament to create with no income coming in." Her next disc? ('Records', Pym calls them.) "I'd like the voice of somebody I know on this island." She chooses "An Arundel Tomb" by Philip Larkin. His deep boot-toned voice reverberates, with the last re-assuring words "what will survive of us is love". The pre-Baroque tomb of a nobleman and his lady had reclined through the centuries with their dogs poignantly curled at their feet. Larkin wrote and congratulated her for speaking 'very sensibly and amusingly'. He was honoured to be included with his reading, "though I could hardly bear my tedious voice slogging on".

We are next reminded that in 1963, Pym had her seventh novel rejected: "My style of writing was not wanted in the "swinging sixties"."

"Did you change your style?"

"No, but I adopted a man's name – but the novel inside was still the same. My books were now UNSALEABLE."

After sixteen years in the cold, Pym was cited twice as the most under-rated writer for seventy five years.

"Who is she they all wanted to know! – I actually had a new novel ready for a new publisher – Macmillan."

Pym now imagines a storm on the island. "A splendid piece of organ music to drown the thunder is what I feel I need." Strong strident and consoling, Messiaen's opening to *Les Enfants de Dieu, La Nativité du Seigneur* rolls in.

"Your book *The Sweet Dove Died* has just been published?"

"A more contemporary subject. I was interested in the relationship of an older woman and a younger man. I felt it had not been written about."

"Anything at the moment?"

"Yes, I am working on it. But I am busy in retirement and find many things to do. Just twelve miles from Oxford and the nice country all around … I am not as disciplined a writer as I should like. I try to write every morning. I keep note books of everything. Two pages typed of 800 words in a morning and I am quite pleased with myself."

"The next record is in memory of my first holiday in Greece in 1964." She and Hilary shared a love of Greece and Greek songs. She chose a song by Mikis Theodorakis – "Sto Perigiali". A man and a woman walk by the seashore when he stoops to write 'I love you' on the sand. To his sadness, the words are washed away by the sea.

How would she manage on the island?

"I would make a shelter contrived with leaves and branches. I am fond of cooking and sewing." She would make no attempt to escape. She was too frightened of the sea.

For her seventh record Pym chooses Johann Strauss' "Czardas" from the second act of *Fledermaus*; the Hungarian dance that starts slowly and ends with a wild flourish. Pym has never been to Vienna but likes to evoke that old-Vienna romantic period; indeed her own pre-war romantic encounters in Eastern Europe. "Sung or played?" "PLAYED."

"If I was on the island over Christmas I would like a carol – "In the Bleak Mid Winter" by Christina Rossetti, sung by King's College, Cambridge." And which disc would she choose for the island?

"I will take the last one – 'In the Bleak Mid Winter' "

"And your luxury?"

"A case of white wine – would a case be washed ashore, do you think?" she asks playfully.

"German, French, Spanish?" – "German, please."

She chooses Henry James' *The Golden Bowl* for her book. It was James' last novel and has the distinction of being his only novel that ends well for his characters. Pamela Howe later referred to Pym's choice as 'inscrutable'; she herself would take Pym's 'books for a bad day' to the desert island.

Pym thanks Plomley warmly. "I only hope that the casting away will be as nice as the talking about it has been."

Pym's morale had been further boosted in October 1978 when she was elected a Fellow of the Royal Society of Literature. She had also been invited to 'Feasts' at Oxford's University College and at Rawlinson College at St John's. Such disparate luminaries as Lord Goodman, Harold Wilson and Stephen Spender had been fellow guests. Pym spent the night in college, where the niceties of bedside lamps and a bottle of Malvern water had impressed her. After managing a substantial breakfast of bacon and eggs, she was driven to the station by the handsome young High Mistress, Mrs Heather Brigstocke, of St Paul's Girls' School in her Daimler. Combining the two evenings, Pym wrote a short story for *The New Yorker* – "Across a Crowded Room"; considered by Hazel Holt, "a delicately balanced piece ... one of the most satisfying of all her short stories." But with "her sprinkles of rue" (as always termed by Harvey) any vestige of romance was wiped out, with the middle-aged heroine aware that her old admirer had scarcely remembered her.

Pym was now increasingly conscious that she was becoming seriously unwell. In January 1979 she talked with her doctor about her unnatural weight gain. He gave a vague and perplexing prognosis and booked her an appointment with a consultant surgeon in Oxford. Fluid in her abdomen was suspected and a week in the Churchill was advised. Pym was grimly accepting the tentative analysis of something malignant in the abdomen area. But the X-rays were not conclusive, and she was altogether relieved; relieved and "even euphoric" that she had addressed her problem. She knew now that she was dying; that the mooted 'ovarian problem' would be treated with drugs and injections as mere palliatives. There was no cure for her. She took her pleasures cautiously and well-filtered. With the swings and roundabouts of remission, she felt better by February. She wrote optimistically to Bob Smith in Ibadan, that she expected "a few more years of good life". In March she went to "Hatchards, Authors of the Year Party"; her new literary profile led to introductions with Olivia Manning, Iris Murdoch and the Revd. W Baddeley of St James's, Piccadilly. "The Duke of Edinburgh was there but I don't think he reads my books," she reported on the scene in a letter to Larkin. She again steeled herself for another day in London, at "The Romantic Novelists' lunch at the Park Lane Hotel. She had been more amused by the vast basement ladies cloakroom. "With marble basins and pink velvet sofas." Taking a bus to Paddington, she had time to take tea in the Refreshment room on Platform 1; "a quiet calm of mind all passion spent tea", to collect her thoughts and perhaps recall those favourite lines of Wordsworth: "Poetry is the spontaneous overflow of powerful feelings: it takes its origin from emotion recollected in tranquillity." She was relieved to be back home again in the country.

The small things mattered; with Minerva's assisted death in March, a 'spherical' tabby cat had adopted them. Four kittens were born – "all Toms!" Children from the village flocked to see them. Pym was enjoying life – or was it her remission? The intravenous cytotoxic drug, Thiotepa, used in treatment of cancer of the bladder and ovary gave her no bad effects ... for the moment. After one session at the Churchill radio-therapy unit she even ate "a large lunch at The Gate of India in Oxford". On a lush, damp, green

May evening they heard the cuckoo ... "summer at last! (what one has stayed alive for?!)" She noted on June 2nd in her diary, a single line. "I am now in my 67th year – shall I make 70?"

She and Hilary spent three lovely sunny days at Snape and Aldeburgh. A new novel was simmering in her mind through that last summer. A page from her final note book – dated 24.6.79 delineates a plot:

> In this new novel there will be two women starting with their college lives (not earlier) one from a privileged background, the other from a more ordinary one (but not working class) and the subsequent course of their lives ...

She was particularly flattered with her growing following in the USA and was amused, as she languished in the garden, to receive an invitation to lecture in Carlisle, Pennsylvania. A charming letter had also come from a man in Boston, who wanted her "literary remains". Earlier in the year she had had another surprise letter from one Nancy Talburt, Professor of English at the University of Arkansas. Could they meet? Pym happily accepted an invitation for lunch at the Randolph Hotel. She carried an inscribed copy of *Some Tame Gazelle* in her string bag as identification. "Novelists are, on the whole, rather disappointing face to face," she had warned her hostess. She insisted on buying them both gins and tonics at the bar, when Talburt had fondly imagined she would opt for sherry. During their sumptuous lunch, starting from a huge choice of hors d'oeuvres and ending with gooseberry tart and cream, Pym and her elegant companion talked widely; from Oxford, English Literature, anthropology, Naples, sister Hilary's translation of Greek folk songs, to E M Forster and the differing views he brings upon himself. They both favoured the same best London restaurants: The White Tower and Kettners. Pym assured Talburt that she liked American reviewers – particularly John Updike; they were more sympathetic than the British. And she admired their writer, Alison Lurie. To Talburt, she had appeared young and healthy and "had a warm crooked smile and was somebody that one would instantly like to know". Certainly, when lunching in early July, at her old Oxford College, St Hilda's, Pym had felt comparatively younger and slimmer than some of her contemporaries.

But by "July 22nd – Sunday. Dull day. I am definitely fatter – is it the fluid again or does the Thiotepa make me fat? The lady doctor at the Churchill says it doesn't seem to be fluid but I am not so sure." By August, as she doggedly typed out her novel, things deteriorated. Her body was blown out again; she felt acutely sick. She recorded her worries and physical misery in her note book; her last note book:

"Perhaps what one fears about dying won't be the actual moment – one hopes – but what you have to go through beforehand – in my case this uncomfortable swollen body and feeling sick and no interest in food or drink." She was taken back into the Churchill radio-therapy ward. She was drained of fluid, taken off Thiotepa and felt no better. The doctors were non committal about the drug's effect. There were "other things" they could try. By October 1st, she reported, in her diary; "I am not feeling well at the moment (more fluid ...)" She now reflected morbidly on the unexplicable mystery of life and death and "the way we all pass through this world in a kind of procession".

Pym was given new tablets; thoroughly weakened by nausea, her lack of appetite, she retired to bed, with nips of brandy, Lucozade, weak tea and toast. Was she reminded of the story she wrote – "An Afternoon Visit"?

Judith started up in horror. Surely Mrs Lacey didn't mean that she was going to die soon ... "Everybody dies," she said uncertainly.

"Yes, but we don't always know when we're going to die, do we? I think I'm rather lucky to know that, though it's a little frightening, too." Mrs Lacey drew the collar of her mauve chiffon bed-jacket a little closer round her neck.

The unusually hot October sun poured through Pym's bedroom, until she found it too strong and drew her curtains. (It occurred to her the windows needed cleaning ... .) She was cheered by her doctor's visits. He now pre-scribed champagne. Larkin's last letters to her were solicitous, charming, humorous and characteristically self-deprecating.

Ist November 1979 – I'm so sorry you're not so well. Perhaps the new drug is taking away your appetite, as a side effect. It was good of you to write. Can you 'work' in bed? But perhaps you don't want to ... 'breakfast in bed' is a hardship for me, balancing and biting precariously ... I do hope you feel better soon, perhaps even by the time you get this. Wd [*sic*] Hilary mind if I rang up some evening next week to ask after you? Anyway, please don't feel you must answer this, although of course it's always a pleasure and privilege to hear from you …

With all good wishes,
Yours ever, Philip.

It became apparent to Pym that she would soon become a burden to Hilary. On November 5th, she had written to Bob Smith. ("Barbara's last letter to me" is written at the page's head).

"Dearest Bob, Thank you so much for your nice long letter, written on that nice club paper*. I came back from my three-day hospital stay on Saturday afternoon – Hilary collected me of course and I managed to totter into the car. I can't honestly say that I feel much better at the moment as they have given me more and different drugs, which they hope will 'do something' but I suppose I must be patient." She continued in a light vein, full of literary and churchy news and with enquiries after his work at The Church Union. "Hilary has got some quarter bottles of champagne for me which should revive me, and our vicar also gave me a bottle."

Together with Hilary, who had tended her with constant cheer and affection, Pym was shown round a hospice near Oxford. From her wheelchair she immediately spotted 'material'. It was arranged she would move in after Christmas. She sent Larkin a card (sold in aid of the Protection of Rural England) of a winter sun setting over fields and hedges thick with snow.

Still struggling on – perhaps a little better! Another visit to hospital (brief) on 2nd Jan.

Barbara

---

* (The Professor is a member of The Oxford and Cambridge Club)

Her life was in order. She had entrusted her close friend and executor, Hazel Holt, to see *A Few Green Leaves* 'through the press'. She was ready for death. Henry Harvey was with her, just two days before she died: "We had great fun. Her spirit was high."

She died in the morning of January 11th, 1980.

Postscript: Oswestry WW1–1980

Barbara's birth place at 72 Willow Street was replaced with a substantial block of flats in 1985. By the year 2002, the adjoining house was in a derelict state, with 'junkie dwelling' scrawled across its front wall. A smashed door pane exuded a fetid stench from its stygian interior. The remaining terrace with wide-arched Edwardian windows, together with a variety of 18th and 19th century houses, slopes down the street to the town centre, The Cross. By 1916, the year of Hilary's birth, the family had moved from their lodgings to a small detached house nearby, in Welsh Walls. But it was at Morda Lodge, their spacious Edwardian home from around 1920, that family life unfolded through to World War Two.

The name Oswestry – from Oswald's tree – harks back fifteen centuries to the Northumbrian King, St Oswald, who was nailed to a tree by the Welsh. St Oswald's Church, in the centre of the town, is a sturdy mongrel of the medieval, with Victorian embellishments. The buttressed Gothic tower is capped by eight fine and ancient pinnacles. 'Assistant Dogs Only Please!' is advised on the inner door. Across the glowing Victorian floor tiles, a spacious maze of aisles is revealed, dabbed with colour from a phalanx of Victorian stained-glass windows.

'To the Glory of God and in loving memory – Her Majesty Queen Elizabeth, the Queen Mother'. By the Lady's Chapel in that early April 2002, a small table had been set up with a vase of white rosebuds, a scented candle and an invitation to sign a book of remembrance (Her Majesty had been a staunch fan of Barbara Pym). Beside the church an ancient wood lych gate and a pair of fine 18th-century wrought iron gates further guarded her rest.

In the secluded north chapel of St Catherine, set aside for 'quiet prayer', I sat on the polished oak organ stool. Here the little girls' mother, Irena Pym, in her capacity as assistant organist, would practise and play her canticles, psalms and glorias. Hilary remembered how they would squeeze up along-side, their eyes glued to the console, watching the intricacies of the keys and stops. Each ivory head to its function: 'Swell sub octave' – 'Unison off – 'Acoustic Bass' – 'Horn' – 'Oboe' – 'Vox angelica' – 'Dulciana'. Meanwhile the Parish News portrayed a commitment to Social Church activity that closely emulated the Pym family's parameters of eighty years ago. The rota for the Church Flowers (a detail which featured regularly in Pym's earlier novels) – Coffee Rota – Men's Breakfast – Ladies Group – Church cleaning co-ordinator – Ministry of welcome – Friends of the music . . .

A few hundred yards west of St Oswald's along Church Street, stands Morda Lodge. Approached by a terrace of artisans' cottages – one with 'Round the Back' pinned to its front street door and emitting a fury of sawing and hammering – and a contingent of Victorian villas. Their ornate timber-framed gables and massive chimneys loom behind high walls, clus-tered with scarlet japonica and scented choisya. Morda Lodge, standing well back from the road, is masked by a fine yew hedge. Embedded in the stone entrance wall is a discreet metal plaque: 'The Home of Barbara Pym, Novelist (1913–1980)' as directed by the Local Heritage Society. A big, tall house, its once sombre red brick façades are now painted cream with an emerald front door. A free-standing arch to the left leads to a deep garden, sheltered by towering Scots pine and conifers, a spreading willow and two tall cherry trees in the far centre lawn. In early 1938 Barbara wrote from Morda Lodge, in a combined letter to Robert Liddell, Henry and Elsie Harvey, in Helsingfors: 'Now it is spring and the garden is full of beautiful flowers, primroses, violets, daffodils, scyllas, grape hyacinths, anemones und so weiter . . .' She next described the old brown horse in the paddock beside the house walking slowly, majestically. At the ripe age of twenty-five years and purporting to be disappointed in love, she makes for playful analogy between 'this so dull spinster, which is like the old brown horse.' She continues her blithe soliloquy: 'And the cherry tree at the bottom of the garden is out, and Miss Pym, this learned old spinster, is quoting A E Housman to herself, and she is picking flowers to put in her room and she is wearing a black jersey and sandals . . .'

Standing today beside the tall cherry tree as it sways in the breeze, we remember how Barbara sat just here, in her green deck chair, reading Byron's 'Don Juan', smoking her Russian cigarette and turning her face to the sun. But that three-acre green sweep of paddock is no more.

It is the province of bungalows and trim gardens. We come to the back yard and the window ledge where Barbara sat in her newly made 'orangey-pink and white check gingham, $5\frac{3}{4}$d a yard.' The coach house converted garage still exists. 'Those girls can't have had much room to play, in that old loft' said my host and led the way into the house. His wife was from Thailand. A discreet display of gilded Buddhas adorned the interior to include the extant billiard room in the attic. Barbara's mother could never have sustained any such Eastern accoutrements alongside her fond nurture of the young curates. The house is light and spacious with little changed since the Pym family's tenure. The drawing room to the left of the entrance hall, where Aunt Janie sat knitting her white jumper that went all wrong and Barbara, sitting opposite, knitted her pink one. The dining room to the right is high-ceilinged like all the ground-floor rooms, with wide bay windows. The walls throughout have retained their original anaglypta and are painted over, pale yellow, rose and ochre. It was in this dining room that the new curates were given a ritual boiled chicken for dinner, smothered in a white sauce. There is no mention of wine accompanying these artless suppers. Instead tea trays with home-made sponge cake and hot milky bedtime drinks take precedence in Barbara's fictive agendas. In an attempt to inject some drama into the drawing room of her first novel – *Some Tame Gazelle* – she had staged a morning proposal of marriage. The local deputy librarian declared his love and troth for the handsome and socially superior Harriet. She rebuffed him graciously and he was considerably mollified to note he had plenty of time for a visit to the Crownwheel and Pinion before lunch... My host was talking: 'They had no electricity on the second floor and only one bathroom.' We stepped down to the kitchen and scullery and to the extensive stone cellar, where Irena's spring bulbs, planted in bowls, were left for their shoots to sprout and where the cats all slept at night.

With her acute eye to social and racial change, Barbara, from her early novels in the 1950s, would include some amiable alien to colour her portrayals of the quiet life. In *Civil to Strangers*, the Hungarian, Stefan Tilos, pines in Shropshire for his wild boar hunting. He turns his attentions instead to the beautiful Cassandra with bunches of lilies and a full-blooded flirtation. And in *No Fond Return of Love*, the unctuous Brazilian, Senhor Macbride-Pereira, idles at his window and marvels at the 'the things I see'. It would not surprise Barbara that a Thai lady now ran her old family home and that an authoritative Indian had opened the door on to her old school.

School holidays from Huyton accentuated the amenities of Oswestry as much as the spectacular surrounding country. Despite bicycling through the steep cliffs of Llanymynech Hill, walking, picnicking and golf practice, the teenage sisters were drawn to the Regal cinema. There was a change of programme twice a week. Its grand pillared entrance, set on a rotunda, must have presaged every promise. Today, its 1930s glory is boarded up and abandoned. Along from the Regal, in Leg Street, stood the popular black and white heavily timbered Blackgate Café. Here Barbara met her girlfriends for coffee. Dark and cosy, it was the perfect venue for confidences. Hilary aged 14 years and fat and shy would tag along. She remembered the Vicar's daughter was especially racy. "I think I have an inferiority complex" she pleaded one day. Replied Barbara hastily? "Even if you have, it's not the kind of thing you discuss in public." A pub today and probably even more conducive to convivial exchange. Another hypnotic point of interest for Barbara was the Midland Bank. Built in 1890, it boasts a phalanx of tall, mullioned windows at ground level, to invite a glance inside. Barbara aged 16 years had conceived her first passion; a young bank clerk was incarcerated within this imposing place of work. In trepidation she would pass non-chalantly along the pavement by the high windows, straining to glimpse her hero 'at his post on the concourse. Her infatuation was increased by his regular performance as a lay reader. She sat in church, enthralled at his voice, his spirituality and his beauty, as framed against the autumnal background of Harvest Festival. Barbara gave vent to her unwitting swain in a poem, entitled 'Midland Bank'. Hilary always remembered the first two lines:

In the cool sanctity of Midland Bank
I see the clerks, pale fishes in the Tank.

Such fruitful intrigue and emotion could not go wasting. The young clerk was duly resurrected in her novel *Jane and Prudence*. Re-cast as Mr Oliver, he was invited to tea at the vicarage. The conversation between himself and mother and daughter was stilted. It must be so interesting working in a bank – was he shut up in a room at the back? Could he be seen over the counter? ' "No, I am not visible to passers-by" said Mr Oliver with a faint smile.' Flora, now confronted with her paragon, was lost for words. Her feelings for him were waning. That initial flood of love for him, when, distanced at the church he had read the lessons, was floundering. ' "I am going up to Oxford next week," said Flora, to break the silence.'

When Barbara herself went up to Oxford and made new sophisticated and well travelled friends, she felt inhibited by Oswestry and her quiet, parochial upbringing. However a few ardent admirers made the pilgrimage to Morda Lodge. Her serious suitor, Rupert Gleadow, had stayed a whole week in September 1932 and found Oswestry a pleasant country market town: "quite fit for the honour of your residence."

From the castle ruins on a grass mount, thick with scented white clythera, the eye is carried west to the distant wave of Welsh hills. The panorama below of slate roofs and rose brick church towers and steeples, swathed in meadows, copse and spinney is an inducement to explore further. On September 16th, Rupert and Barbara set off for Llynclys Hill, a five mile drive on the 2 bus, south of Oswestry. Past rolling country of sheep and plough and hedged grazing land, they reached Llanymynech. Taking the twisting stone lanes they walked up through the ancient BC rock hills of limestone, woodland and fish pools. At a rough wooden ladder – Jacob's Ladder – they rested and had lunch. Sipping beer and Dry Ginger they gazed below on woods flung like a shawl around the grazing sheep. Barbara recorded in her diary:

"16th September. We walked up to Llynclys Hill and when up by Jacob's Ladder found a convenient resting place and had our lunch there … we walked up again to the hill and made ourselves com-fortable in the sun. We lay half asleep with our faces close to each other for a long time …"

Barbara described it as "a heavenly week together". They had, she wrote, "laughed out of sheer happiness". She had tried to persuade Rupert that any happiness in love was worth the unhappiness it might bring. As his entreaties to make love to her at the end of their week together had been robustly repudiated, Rupert was non-plussed. He later wrote ruefully: "... I have never felt for <u>anyone</u> ... such feelings as I have felt for you – and still do feel" and finally conceded: "Perhaps I should have said your emotions never run away with you: your sympathies do not come flowing out of a soft heart ..."

Rupert Gleadow embodied Barbara's closest chance of marriage. They always stayed friends. She enjoyed his second wife, Helen – a vivacious blue-eyed blonde – and would visit them in their Chelsea home.

On one memorable day in August 1935 Harvey and Liddell came to see her at Morda Lodge. "It was lovely" trilled Barbara. "Henry was absolutely at his best. He wore his grey flannel suit, a bright blue silk shirt with a darker blue tie and blue socks." Liddell and a third Oxford friend, John Barnicot, both appeared equally formal. As they all sat in a bosky corner of the garden, chatting and smoking, Pym looked radiant and supreme; a veritable lioness with her pride. Her own cotton dress was stitched with prominent kisses at the neck and breast and waist. Her coquettish appearance had even induced Henry to take her in his arms in the bathroom and in her bedroom. When in the evening they left for Oxford, he had tried to persuade her to come with them. She noted: "I feel it is better that I remain here, thinking lovingly of him with more real fondness than before." He was due to take up his teaching post in Helsingfors just two weeks later. The longing and languor set in. "No letter from Henry" she recorded on November 10th. In January 1936 he finally wrote her a long letter in Latin, German, French, Swedish, Finnish ...

Select Bibliography

PRIMARY SOURCES

Some Tame Gazelle
Excellent Women
Jane and Prudence
Less than Angels
A Glass of Blessings
No Fond Return of Love
Quartet in Autumn
The Sweet Dove Died
A Few Green Leaves (Posthumous)
An Unsuitable Attachment (Posthumous)
Crampton Hodnet (Posthumous)
An Academic Question (Posthumous)
Young Men in Fancy Dress (Unpublished)

SECONDARY SOURCES

ACKROYD Peter, Review of *The Sweet Dove Died*, *The Sunday Times* 16.7.78
ADAMSON Lesley, 'GUARDIAN WOMEN', *The Guardian*
AFRICA – Quarterly Journal of The International African Institute, edited by Professor Daryll Forde
BBC – National Sound Archives
BBC – Written Archives
BBC – Radio 3 *Finding a Voice* recording by Barbara Pym

BETJEMAN Sir John, *An Oxford University Chest*

BINDING Paul, *Barbara Pym – British Novelists Since 1960* (Dictionary of Literary Biography)

THE BODLEIAN LIBRARY Room 132

THE BRITISH LIBRARY

BURKHART Charles, *The Pleasure of Miss Pym*

CAMBRIDGE University Library

CECIL, Lord David, *A Portrait of Jane Austen*

COLINDALE Newspaper Library

COMPTON-BURNETT Dame Ivy, *More Women Than Men*

CORNHILL Magazine

GASCOIGNE Bamber, *Encyclopedia of Britain*

GLENDINNING Victoria, Review of *Quartet in Autumn* – 'The Best High Comedy'. *The New York Times*

GREEN LEAVES, The Journal of the Barbara Pym Society

HOLT Hazel, *A Lot to Ask – a Life of Barbara Pym*

HOWE Pamela, 'The cruelly perceptive eye of a born novelist', *The Listener*

HUXLEY Aldous, *Crome Yellow*

INTERNATIONAL AFRICAN INSTITUTE, SOAS, University of London

JAMES Henry, *The Golden Bowl*

KING Francis, 'Out of Sight' – 'Francis King talks to novelist Robert Liddell' in *Gay Times*

LARKIN Philip, *Further Requirement – 'Interviews, Broadcasts, Statements and Book Reviews'* – 'The World of Barbara Pym', *The Times Literary Supplement*

LIDDELL Robert, *A Mind at Ease* – Barbara Pym and Her Novels, and 'A Success Story' – Contribution to *The Life and Work of Barbara Pym* edited by Dale Salwak

MOOREHEAD Caroline, 'How Barbara Pym was Rediscovered after 16 years out in the Cold', *The Times* 14.9.77

THE NEW YORK TIMES, Reviews

THE NEW YORKER, Short Stories

PEVSNER Nikolaus, *London 1, London 2-South*, and *Oxfordshire*

PITKIN, Church Guides

PLOMLEY Roy, *Desert Island Discs* 29.7.78

PYM Barbara, '*A Very Private Eye*, an autobiography in Diaries and Letters' by Hazel Holt and Hilary Pym

THE REDWOOD LIBRARY, Newport, Rhode Island, USA

ROSSEN Janice, 'Love in the Great Libraries: Oxford in the work of Barbara Pym', *Journal of Modern Literature*

ROWSE, A.L., 'Miss Pym and Miss Austen'. Contribution to *The Life and Work of Barbara Pym* edited by Dale Salwak

RUNCIE James, Script of *Miss Pym's Day Out* transmitted by BBC Television 29.2.92

SALVE REGINA UNIVERSITY, McKillop Library, Newport, Rhode Island, USA

SALWAK Dale, Editor: *The Life and Work of Barbara Pym*

SHROPSHIRE WILDLIFE TRUST

SMITH Robert (Prof), (1) 'Always Sincere; Not Always Serious – Robert Liddell and Barbara Pym', *Twentieth Century Literature*

(2) 'How Pleasant to Know Miss Pym', *ARIEL*

THE SUNDAY TELEGRAPH, Reviews and articles

THE SUNDAY TIMES, Reviews and articles

LITERARY REVIEW

THE *TIMES LITERARY SUPPLEMENT*

UNIVERSITY OF Rhode Island

WELCH Denton, *Maiden Voyage*

WYNDHAM Francis, 'The Gentle Power of Barbara Pym', *The Sunday Times*

Index

This index was compiled by Douglas Matthews.